Beauty Therapist

TO

ENTREPRENEUR

The essential guide to
accelerating your career success
in the beauty industry

LINDA HILL

R∃THINK PRESS

First published in Great Britain in 2019 by Rethink Press
(www.rethinkpress.com)

This book is dedicated to my dad, Charlie, who is truly remarkable and one of the most inspiring people I know. He taught me that you can do anything you set your mind to. What a wonderful gift to give your child, and for this, I am truly grateful.

Contents

The back story

I was thirteen when I decided the school I was in wasn't the right one for me. It was a great school, included in the University of Cambridge's *Guide to Excellence*, which outlines the top 100 schools worldwide. To stand out in the school, you had to be very academic, very sporty, or very good looking. I was none of these. I knew if I wanted to excel, I had to change schools.

It's now hard to imagine a world without Google, but back then if you wanted to do research, your choices were either the Yellow Pages or an encyclopaedia. Armed with the Yellow Pages, I decided to find a new school for myself. My strategy was to pinpoint an area and then shortlist three schools. As a way of discouraging me, my mom said if I wanted to change schools I would have to organise everything myself. So, I called the three schools to set up meetings. I figured it was best to meet face-to-face with the housemaster, get a tour of the school, and then make my decision. When I arrived at Paarl Girls' High, set at the bottom of the Paarl Mountain, my gut told me this was *the* one.

The process of choosing my own school taught me that if you aren't happy with your circumstances, you must find a way to change them or you must accept them and get on with it.

During my final year of high school, I was constantly asked 'What are you going to do next year?' My plan was to go to a finishing school in Switzerland. My dad cleverly asked me if I'd considered enlisting in the army instead. He went on to say that it would be a similar experience and great preparation for the real world. I didn't think there would be any similarities, but then came the trump card – only 200 students were chosen each year to attend the South African Army Women's College. This was his way of saying that it would be impossible for me to get in. Always up for a challenge, I soon forgot about Switzerland and my thoughts shifted to how I could be selected as one of the 200 girls.

I wasn't sure how to prepare for the army interview. I only knew that the process, conducted over eight hours, would be comprised of gruelling panel interviews followed by psychometric testing. The questions asked were varied and meant to test character. I remember being asked why I hadn't been selected as head girl and had made it only to prefect. One sergeant asked me why I was overweight; it was more a statement than a question. I remember thinking, 'Speak for yourself.' A few weeks later I learned that I'd been selected. I was over the moon.

For some reason I'd expected the army to be like girl guides or scouts. It was nothing like that, apart from the brown uniform. We learned to shoot with R4 rifles and take our 9 mm pistols apart blindfolded and then put them back together again. Sometimes our platoon would be dropped off in the middle of nowhere with only a compass, map, and water bottle. We were expected to negotiate our way back to base camp.

I learned all sorts of interesting things that year, but the most valuable lesson was this: when circumstances are challenging, camaraderie and staying positive will keep you going. When it was finally time to leave, I was sad to say goodbye to all the great people I'd met but thankful for a year of learning about leadership, teamwork, and dealing with whatever might come my way.

It was now time to start university. My first day was full of promise. I felt so grown-up and confident walking into the Faculty of Education building – until I couldn't find my class. I stopped one of the lecturers and asked him where I could find the Phys Ed students. He looked at me in surprise and said they had discontinued the course. He asked if I had received a letter. I had not.

I asked the lecturer what he taught, and he said art. He went on to explain that it was a four-year teaching degree with a major in art. In that moment I decided that was precisely what I would study. Isn't it amazing how we can take so little time making life-changing decisions and so much time making unimportant ones, such as what to order from the menu or what outfit to wear to a party? During those four years, I learned that if you put your mind to something, you can do it. If you want something badly enough, you will find a way to accomplish it. If not, you will find an excuse.

Towards the end of my time at university, I knew I wanted to see the world. I was fortunate to be accepted into a student exchange programme to the United States. This was a dream come true. That year was one of the best years of my life because every day was an adventure. I met incredible people, bought a van, and travelled across the States and Europe for a year. With no mobile phones or internet, the only way of staying in touch was through post cards and letters. It was simply a case of saying, 'I'll see you in a year from now.' You just had to trust that things would work out. Life is like that too – you have to give it your best shot and trust that it will work out.

When I returned to South Africa, I landed a teaching job at a fantastic school. The kids were well behaved and my colleagues were a great bunch of teachers, all trying to make a difference. I enjoyed the job but after two years, I felt the need to do more, so I decided to study public relations. After I got my diploma I was offered a job, but at the same time, my best friend told me she was going to London and asked if I wanted to join her. I was torn. Here was my opportunity to break into PR and here was also a chance to work abroad. In the end, Ralph Waldo Emerson's words helped me to make my decision.

'Do not go where the path may lead, go instead where there is no path and leave a trail.'

Sometimes circumstances force us to sidestep the career ladder and go somewhere a little more scenic. Embrace these detours. They're just as important as the upward movement. They make us stronger and more resilient, and the further up the ladder we get, the stronger and more resilient we need to be.

Teaching in London was challenging. Every day I went to a different school, into a different class, to teach a different group of kids. I spent hours at night making beautiful worksheets. Early in the morning I'd go to the newsagent to photocopy them. These were the days before home printers. Some of the kids took one look at the worksheet, looked at me, and then ripped it up. The day a young child tried to stab me was the day I decided to change careers. I enrolled in a CIBTAC and CIDESCO beauty course.

I was lucky to get my first beauty job while I was still a student. It wasn't easy going to college during the day and working at a beauty salon evenings and weekends. For extra money I would waitress, too. Sometimes we just have to make sacrifices to get closer to our goal, whatever that might be.

Next, I worked in a beautiful spa. It was completely different from the neighbourhood salon. Not only did I learn a host of new treatments here, but I also made incredible friendships. The experience taught me that the environment, culture, and people we surround ourselves with have a huge impact on our happiness at work.

I then landed a role as a beauty lecturer at a college in London teaching NVQ, CIBTAC, and CIDESCO students. It was challenging and rewarding in equal measure. The students I stayed in touch with went on to excel in their careers. What set them apart was choice. They chose to make the most of each learning opportunity and chose to put in the work.

From there, I went on to work for a five-star hotel group. Treating A-list celebrities was the norm at the hotel. The ones who stood out were the ones who were kind and humble despite their fame.

Next, I was headhunted for a position as beauty manager for a health club group. This was my first experience recruiting staff. Every so often someone would apply who didn't have quite the right skills or experience but had something else – the right attitude, work ethic, and drive. These are the ones who go far. I ended up as acting general manager of the health club. What an experience this was, dealing with all sorts of enquiries and complaints on a daily basis. What I realised was that you can never satisfy everyone. It's better to attract customers who love what you do and value what you have to offer than to try to be everything to everyone.

In 2004, I set up an aesthetic and beauty recruitment business. This was a natural progression in an industry I knew so well. This book was inspired by my desire to share all the best practices that I've acquired over many years of working with thousands of salons, clinics, and spas. It will help to accelerate your successes and fast-track your career in this exciting and ever-changing industry.

PART ONE

GETTING STARTED

CHAPTER ONE

The Catch-22

You've just finished your studies and need to find your first job in the beauty industry. Most employers are looking for experience, and most of the online job ads list experience as one of their requirements. How do you overcome this dilemma when nobody is willing to give you a chance?

Getting a job when you have no experience

Step one: be flexible

Be more flexible. To stand out, tell companies that you're willing to work evenings and weekends and start at the bottom. The more experienced candidates no longer want to work evenings and weekends, so blow the competition out of the water. Position yourself as someone who is flexible and willing to work the shifts that others no longer want.

If you have the flexibility to accept a lower salary, this will also help you secure a job faster. Often companies don't have the time or resources to invest in training and would prefer someone who is already trained. If you make it clear that you can afford a lower salary in the short term while you prove yourself, you will catch the employer's attention. Don't let your ego get in the way. You know you're worth more but just need a break to show an employer how good you are. If you've come from a different industry, be prepared to take a salary cut to get your foot in the door.

Step two: ask for recommendation letters

If this is your first job, ask your college lecturer to write a letter of recommendation for you. Sending a recommendation letter with your job application will make you stand out. If others are singing your praises, this will give a potential employer peace of mind. If you've had previous jobs, ask your last two employers if they would be willing to write a letter of recommendation for you. Letters are much more powerful than just the names and contact details of your referees.

Step three: determine your ideal environment

Decide what type of environment you would like to work in. Have a think about your strengths and weaknesses and what type of environment would suit you best. Would you love to work in a boutique salon? Or would you prefer a bigger hotel environment? Do you like structure or do you prefer a more relaxed environment? Perhaps you enjoy the buzz of busy retail counters in department stores? Find the opportunity for work experience in the environment in which you envision yourself. By shadowing others and helping out, you'll not only build experience but will also have the opportunity to request a reference upon completion. During this time, make a point of going the extra mile.

Step four: network

Network as much as possible. This means telling people that you're looking for a new position. Ask people if they know anyone in the beauty industry who might be able to help you or point you in the right direction. Word of mouth is extremely powerful. If someone else refers you, you're already ahead of the competition, having been given the seal of approval by at least one professional.

Step five: create a CV and cover letter

Ensure your CV includes the *big five*:

- Contact details
- Personal profile
- Education
- Work history
- Interests and hobbies

Spend time crafting your CV to give yourself the best possible chance to get the job you want. Use the step-by-step guide in Chapter Two to help you write a great cover letter and CV. These will make you stand out from the competition.

Step six: make a shortlist

Write down a list of all the places where you'd like to work. Then, see which ones are feasible in terms of travel and cross off those that don't qualify. The next step is to contact the companies to ask who is in charge of their recruitment. Say that you would like to send them your CV and want to address your letter to the correct person. If you just address the CV to Dear Sir/Madam, it will show you haven't gone the extra mile. Find out the name and email address of the person who deals with recruitment.

Once you have this information, tailor your cover letter and CV to each company. Keep track of where you've sent your CV and the responses. Another option is to make a short pitch video (instead of a cover letter). In this video, share the same information as you would in a cover letter. Explain who you are, what you're looking for, and what attributes you have that would make you a valuable team member.

Chapter Two shows you exactly what information to include in your cover letter or pitch video. Make sure you read Chapter Three as well, as it provides tips on video interviews, which will be useful when you record your pitch video.

Don't be discouraged if you don't hear back straight away. Keep working on your list.

Step seven: take action

Looking for a job can be a full-time job in itself, so you need to be committed to the task. Make sure you explore all avenues. Another option is to turn up in person. This is especially effective with smaller companies that are owner managed.

Print your CV and your cover letter. Dress smartly, as you would for an interview. Ask to speak with the owner or manager when you arrive. Ensure your CV is in an envelope with the manager's or owner's name on it. If the owner or manager isn't available, ask the front of house person if you can leave your CV with them or ask when would be the best time to come back.

Make sure to follow up. Call the salon, clinic, or spa and ask to speak to the person to whom you addressed the CV. Check that they have received it and ask if they are currently recruiting. If they say 'tell us a little more about yourself', use your well-written cover letter as a guide. It'll remind the person what you studied, what experience you have, what you're looking for, and what qualities you would bring to the business.

What nobody tells you when you start out

The number one thing you need to know is that selling is part of your job. Your ability to sell will have a huge impact on your success. Without sales, there will be no job and no business. The selling starts when you apply for the job, as you have to sell yourself to the company. You must convince them that you're the best fit by highlighting all your strengths so that they choose you rather than someone else.

You may have more selling experience than you think. We sell on a daily basis to our friends when we recommend apps to download, films to watch, or places to visit. Our friends buy things because of our recommendations. The key is to see it as prescribing and advising rather than selling. If you aren't confident about your selling ability, consider this: Why do we find it so easy to recommend a product or service to family or friends? Because we think the product or service is great and we want them to benefit from it too. Apply this principle to selling so that your clients will benefit from your treatments and products and ultimately get the best results.

Therapists often think they'll ruin a treatment by selling to their clients. This will be the case if you hard-sell to them. In other words, don't sell just for the sake of it. Selling with integrity is the key to retailing. This is how you build trust. If you sell with enthusiasm, sincerity, and the belief that the product is a great investment, then your clients will buy.

Another thing that nobody really mentions is that working in the beauty industry is incredibly hard work. You may be utterly surprised by the amount of anatomy and physiology you have to master and the list of contraindications you have to memorise. Nobody will prepare you for the back-to-back treatments, the physical endurance, and the emotional fatigue you'll confront every day. Be mindful of your posture so you don't end up with injuries. Clients sometimes pour out their hearts during a treatment, leaving you tired and drained. Ensure that their negative energy doesn't rub off on you. Be a good listener but keep what your clients tell you confidential. You want to create healthy boundaries and act professionally at all times.

In this industry, you have to stay cool, calm, and collected at all times. You need to set the tone in the treatment room so that clients feel safe, relaxed, and in good hands. You can't let on to the clients that behind the scenes, it's not nearly as tranquil as they might think. I once worked in a spa where clients frequently commented that it must be a wonderful place to work because of how peaceful it was. If only they knew! We rushed from one treatment room to another to make sure we ran on time. None of us had our own treatment room, so the changeovers had to be executed with military precision. The prep room was hectic, with therapists mixing products and getting everything ready for their next treatment. However, without fail, every client mentioned the spa's serenity. Whether you work as a therapist, front of house staff, or in a management position, you help set the tone of the salon, spa, or clinic.

The ability to read clients is an advantage – if you're able to pick up on their body language, this will result in greater client satisfaction. Take the subtle hints. Are they feeling uncomfortable? Are they trying to make small talk? Give clients permission to relax and switch off. You can tell them it's their time to unwind so they don't feel they need to make conversation.

The power of your network will have an influence on your success. Start by joining trade and professional associations. Exchanging knowledge and collaborating with other industry professionals will enhance your career. Contact us to receive a coupon with download instructions and get your free copy of our list of trade and professional associations.

www.lindahillrecruitment.co.uk/contact-us

What happens at the trade test

The function of a trade test is to determine your training needs and the standard of your treatments. If you're required to do one, it's best to wear your uniform with flat, closed shoes and your hair tied up, if long. Ensure your nails are short, clean, and varnish free. Present yourself the same way you did for your practical exams.

Hiring managers will test you on the treatments popular in their company. In hotels, it will most likely be a back massage. Salons might test a range of treatments, including waxing, facial cleanse and massage, and file and polish.

You won't know in advance what treatments they'll expect you to do. When preparing for the trade test, plan in which order you'll do the treatments if asked to do more than one.

The first thing to do is ask if you can wash your hands. This will signal to the interviewer that you're focused on hygiene and that your treatments will commence with clean hands.

The trick is to pretend that the interviewer is a client who is having the treatment for the first time. This means that you'll have to explain exactly what you expect of them and what exactly will happen during the treatment.

Back massage

Start by saying to the interviewer that you'll leave the room while they get ready. Tell them exactly what items of clothing need to be removed and how they must position themselves on the treatment couch. Be specific. For example, you might say, 'Lie face down underneath the towel.' Reassure them that there's no rush and you'll be back once they're ready.

Once you return to the treatment room, check that they're warm enough. Adjust the temperature or add a blanket if needed.

Ask questions to ensure it's safe for them to have the treatment and to indicate that you're aware of contraindications. If you're working in a salon, clinic, or spa, the client will have already filled in a consultation form for you to discuss with them.

TIP

Here are some questions you could ask the interviewer.

- What pressure do you like?
- What areas would you like me to concentrate on today?

- Could you be pregnant or are you breastfeeding? (if your interviewer is female)
- Are there any recent injuries or operations I should be aware of?
- Do you have any medical conditions that could affect the treatment?
- Do you suffer from any allergies, such as nut allergies?

Ask the interviewer to let you know if you need to increase or decrease the pressure. Avoid speaking during the massage unless the interviewer engages you in conversation. In college, you may have to follow a set massage routine, but for the trade test, use the information that the interviewer provides to tailor the treatment to them.

When you start the treatment, you might want to leave the towel over the interviewer's back and start off with some pressure points, or you might ask the interviewer to take a few deep breaths. This will help them to relax and calm their mind. Show the interviewer a range of your movements, and if you know any advanced movements (e.g. elbows or forearms) incorporate these as well.

Keep an eye on the time and bring the massage to a close slowly – don't just suddenly stop. Make sure you finish by readjusting the towel over the interviewer's back and doing some stretching moves that will help remove the oil, as you don't want it to stain their clothes.

Offer aftercare advice and tell them that if they were your client, you would suggest booking for regular massages. Finish off the treatment by offering the interviewer a glass of water.

Waxing

Start off by putting on your gloves. Next, test the wax on yourself to ensure the temperature is adequate. You want to make sure the wax is not too hot.

Discard the spatula and the wax strip. Cleanse the area to be waxed and apply the wax in thin, even strokes. Good bonding and stretching will ensure better removal of the wax. Check for stray hairs and remove with tweezers. Now apply your aftercare and give thorough aftercare advice.

Facial cleanse and massage

If you haven't trained with the products, don't worry. The interviewer just wants to feel your hands and see how fluid your moves are. Stick to the cleansing routine you know, unless the interviewer tells you otherwise.

For the massage, have a routine planned that's shorter than your usual one. Often, the interviewer will just want to test you on a five or ten minute massage. Be sure to do fewer repetitions so you have time to showcase a wide range of moves.

Incorporate both the neck and décolleté to make the treatment truly relaxing for the interviewer. Your aim is to make them forget that they're doing a trade test.

File and polish

The interviewer might have really short nails and cuticles that haven't been taken care of. Make no mention of this. Your challenge is to do a flawless paint job, regardless of the state of their nails.

Ask what shape they would like. Once you've done the filing, apply the base coat, two coats of the colour, and finish with the top coat.

Be mindful of the time. Don't make conversation unless the interviewer asks you questions. Focus on your treatment to ensure you get the best result.

After the trade test

The interviewer might give you some feedback straight away, or they might say nothing at all and just bring the interview to a close. Don't say, 'When can I expect to hear from you?' Rather, say, 'Thank you for your time. I look forward to hearing from you.'

CHAPTER TWO

The CV

Having an easy-to-read CV that gives the interviewer an insight into your education, experience and expertise can make the difference between getting an interview or being rejected. You want to make a great first impression so that the interviewer feels compelled to invite you for an interview to find out more about what you can offer their company.

The eight biggest mistakes in your CV

Since 2004, thousands of therapists have sent me their CVs to apply for jobs advertised on our website. Many of these CVs are of poor quality, with important information missing. I find them unclear about the applicants' experience and what roles they're seeking. So, let's look at the eight biggest mistakes people make when crafting their CVs.

Mistake one: not including detailed experience/training

Think about the role you're looking for. If this is a hands-on position (meaning you'll be offering treatments), you must include the treatments you've offered in your previous roles. Often therapists simply write 'All treatments', which is vague. Each salon, spa, and clinic is different, so don't sell yourself short. Be specific. Don't simply write 'facials'; rather, list the individual treatments to show how experienced you are. For example, break it down into microdermabrasion, skin peels, etc. If you don't mention the individual treatments, the potential employer will assume you cannot do them.

List the product houses you've worked with. You'll appear far more valuable to a future employer if they know you're trained in the product houses they use. It will be worth mentioning whether this was in-house or certificate training, as some companies will want you to have a certificate for insurance reasons. If you list 'waxing' as part of your skills but don't mention 'intimate hot waxing', the potential employer will assume you don't offer it. Bear in mind that the reader doesn't know you. You have to make it easy for them to see clearly what treatments you can offer.

Besides listing all the treatments you're confident in providing, also think of other responsibilities you've carried out. Do you perform skin consultations? Advise on products and aftercare depending on your clients' needs? You need to mention this. And don't forget to mention that you sell products and work to targets, if this is the case. It will show the hiring manager that you have experience in retail. Selling is one of a therapist's responsibilities, and if you don't mention this, you are, in fact, saying, 'I'm not doing my job very well.'

If you're applying for a hands-off role in sales, management, or front of house, you still need to mention that you have trained with certain product houses. This shows that you might be able to jump into a treatment in the case of an emergency, and are knowledgeable about products and procedures, both of which are valuable to a potential employer. If the role you're applying for is sales focused, highlight your figures and sales achievements from previous sales positions. This will give the reader insight into your abilities.

The aim of a CV is to sell yourself. Craft one that makes you stand out.

If you're interested in a management role, highlight previous experience that shows you're capable of leading and motivating a team. The reader wants to know that you're capable of inspiring a team and will ultimately drive business and success.

Those applying for front of house roles should draw attention to the fact that they're great at customer service and have previous experience dealing with complaints and working with booking systems, and that they can ensure the smooth running of the front of house.

TIP

When listing your responsibilities, have a look at the job description of the role you're applying for to see if there's an overlap. If there is, make sure you include the relevant responsibilities in your CV.

Mistake two: it has gaps

Hiring managers often scan CVs rather than read them thoroughly, especially when there are many applicants. At a quick glance, they want to see that dates are accounted for and that there are no gaps. Gaps raise questions such as, 'Where were you and what were you up to then?' Hiring managers don't have time to dissect your CV to find out more. Make it easy for them. I always ask candidates why there are gaps in their CV, and the answer is always the same: 'Oh, I didn't think the experiences were relevant to the job I'm applying for.' *Curriculum vitae* is a Latin term which means 'the course of one's life'. All our experiences in life make us who we are. You might find that the seemingly irrelevant experience is what makes you stand out from the crowd.

Therapists often say to me, 'This is my beauty CV. I didn't include everything I did before I studied beauty therapy.' You're not marketing yourself to the fullest if you do this. If you worked in a job where you had to manage people or deal with customers, you gained skills and experience that are transferable to the beauty industry.

If the gaps in your CV relate to travels abroad, mention this. Travelling is one of life's most enriching experiences. While travelling, you're constantly out of your comfort zone, and this helps you become more capable of handling life's challenges. You must deal with new people and different cultures. These experiences are a big bonus when working with clients from different cultures and backgrounds.

Providing all of your experience on your CV can even turn out to be a blessing in disguise. After a year of travelling abroad, I went back to South Africa and started looking for a post as a teacher, keen to get my first job. I sent off fifty applications but missed the boat – all the teachers had already been appointed for the new year. I had lots of experience in the service industry, so I applied for a full-time waitressing role at a nearby coffee shop. In my CV, I included that I'd been to the United States on an exchange programme and was a qualified teacher. I knew I was a good waitress so thought I would have no problem getting the job. I didn't. I'll never forget what the owner told me. She said she was going to do me a favour and not give me the job, not because she thought I wasn't capable but because she thought I needed to do more. I was both disappointed and relieved. If you're ever turned down for a job, it may be a blessing – there may be something better around the corner.

Mistake three: it isn't presented in chronological order

When it comes to listing your education or work history/experience, always mention your most recent position first. No exceptions.

Make it easy for the potential employer to follow your path, so they can get an understanding of what you've achieved along the way. Your CV must flow, and it won't if you don't write it in chronological order.

And if you have a history of job-hopping, you must be twice as impressive in an interview. Owners and managers want to recruit someone whom they can invest in, someone who can grow and develop with the business. Companies that offer training and development opportunities expect employees to use those newly learned skills in their business. If you were at a company for less than a year, this doesn't look good on your CV. Hiring managers are hesitant to even interview a candidate they feel might not have staying power.

You need to send your CV to companies where you feel you can stay and make a difference. This will also give you more job satisfaction. There's nothing worse than being trapped in a job that makes you dread going to work. Don't just send your CV to any company in the hope that they'll take you. You'll be unhappy and get caught up in the job-hopping cycle. The trick is to be selective and committed. Choose carefully.

Mistake four: it's difficult to read

You have to hold the attention of the person reading your CV, so make it easy to read. When writing or updating your CV, refer to the list below.

- Choose one font and stick to it. Don't get creative with the font. Keep it clear and avoid curly typeface.

- Check that your spacing is consistent throughout the document.

- If possible, limit your CV to two pages.

- Use bullet points to list the responsibilities you've held in previous roles.

- Make sure your name and up-to-date contact details are clearly visible at the top of the page.

- Make headings (education, work history, etc.) stand out by underlining them or using bold typeface.

- Present dates consistently. Decide whether you're going to include the months plus the year or just the year.

- Note the dates of your education, including when you started and when you graduated – not just the date you graduated. This will give the reader a clear understanding of how long your courses were.

- Name the company where you worked under your work experience, as well as your job title. This gives the potential employer an instant overview of your experience.

Mistake five: it doesn't include your address

So many of the CVs we receive at our beauty agency don't include an address. If you prefer not to give your full address, at least indicate your area. If you're relocating, use your current address but make it clear you will be relocating, depending on the job offer. If you already know your new address, be sure to include it. If no address is listed, the potential employer will have no idea whether the job you're applying for would even be possible for you in terms of travel.

If you're applying for work in another city or country, state your current location so that interviews will be easier to coordinate (the hiring manager needs to be aware of different time zones).

Mistake six: including a bad photo

A few tips:

- Either look straight at the camera with both shoulders facing the camera or have one shoulder towards the camera and look slightly over it to face the camera

- Keep your hair off your face

- Wear something that looks professional

- Smile and be natural

- Make sure the background isn't distracting

Mistake seven: it doesn't include your interests and hobbies

Why should you include your interests and hobbies in your CV? It gives the interviewer insight into what you enjoy doing outside of work. Life is about balance, and having interests outside of work is healthy. Plus, making time for things you enjoy can help you feel more satisfied at work.

Interests and hobbies can also seal the deal if the interviewer shares some of your passions. Years ago, I pitched for work at a health club chain. They had always worked with another agency. The meeting went well but there was no promise of us working together. Once the meeting was over, the conversation turned to non-work-related topics. The person I'd met with noticed I was wearing a running watch – the type that measures distance and plots your route. She asked if I was a runner. I said I was training for the Stockholm Marathon. Immediately the tone changed. She was a runner, too. We ended up talking about running for the same amount of time as we'd spent talking about business. In the end, the health club happily chose to work with my recruitment agency.

Your interests and hobbies offer a talking point. Recently I interviewed a candidate who was working in a job she didn't enjoy and wanted to get back into the beauty industry. She wanted to combine her administrative skills with front of house duties and work as a clinic coordinator. Her CV said she liked to bake. We started talking about what she enjoyed baking, and her face lit up. She started to relax, and I was able to get a better sense of who she was – someone who was creative, passionate, and a perfectionist. I knew these qualities would serve her well in the role of clinic coordinator. Had we not discussed her interests and hobbies, I'm not sure I would have seen this side of her.

Mistake eight: the profile summary is too long

What's the function of a profile summary at the beginning of your CV?

- It allows you to sell yourself in a few paragraphs

- It gives the reader a quick overview of what type of role you're looking for

- It highlights some of your strengths and provides insight into your character

Your profile summary needs to be short and punchy. If you make it too long, the reader will lose interest. You need to capture their attention just long enough for them to want to read the rest of your CV. Consider an elevator pitch, which requires you to be able to tell someone what you do in the space of a short elevator ride. Think of the profile summary in the same way. You're essentially telling the potential employer who you are, what you're looking for, and why they should employ you.

As with an elevator pitch, the profile summary isn't meant to get you the job. It's meant to pique the reader's interest enough to invite you for an interview. The aim is to get you to the next step. If you're not good at writing, get someone else to write a concise profile summary for you. Review and tweak it until you feel it's a good representation of who you are.

Don't forget to spellcheck your CV and scrutinise it for grammatical errors before you save your final copy.

How to write a great cover letter

When writing your cover letter, your goal should be to make yourself stand out from the competition. As with the profile summary, the cover letter needs to be clear and to the point. Include the following:

- Your qualifications and experience

- What role you're applying for

- The attributes you have that would make you a good fit for the position

- Additional information that reinforces why the company should employ you

EXAMPLE COVER LETTER

Crown House
9 Duke Street
Richmond
TW9 1HP

Louise Smith
The London Boutique Salon
London
SW1A 2RD
1 January 2019

Dear Louise,

I recently graduated from college with a CIDESCO qualification in beauty therapy. I am now looking for my first role within the industry that I am so passionate about. I studied beauty as I love helping others and making a difference.

I am hard-working, honest, and reliable. At my college, I won the Therapist of the Year award, which is given to the student who demonstrates the highest treatment standards and client care, and who has a positive attitude.

Ideally, I am looking for a full-time beauty therapy position where I can build a loyal client base. I can work evenings and weekends and can start immediately. I am flexible with regard to salary, as I am at the start of my career and would love to be given the opportunity to prove myself.

I have previous sales experience, as I worked in a shop whilst at college. During this time, I became confident about selling and I honed my customer-service skills.

Please find attached my CV and a reference letter for you to review.

I look forward to hearing from you, should you have any vacancies now or in future.

Yours sincerely,

Bella Parker

Step-by-step CV writing guide

When you update your CV or draft a new one, ask yourself these questions:

- Does my personal profile highlight my strengths?

- Are my contact details up to date and clearly visible?

- Does my education section start with the most recent?

- Does my work history show the start and finish dates with each company?

- Does my work history include the responsibilities I carried in each role?

- Do my interests and hobbies include activities besides socialising and shopping?

Use the CV template below as a guide, or contact us to receive a coupon with download instructions and get your own copy of the CV template that has helped over 3,000 candidates get their dream job.

www.lindahillrecruitment.co.uk/contact-us

CV TEMPLATE

NAME SURNAME
Curriculum Vitae

Personal Details

Phone:

Email:

Location:

Nationality:

Available starting date:

Summary & Profile

Write a short and concise summary. Use the guidelines in this chapter (mistake eight) to help you craft a punchy profile summary.

Education

Start Date – End Date   Name of College/University
                              Qualification obtained

Start Date – End Date   Name of College/University
                              Qualification obtained

Start Date – End Date   Name of School
                              Qualification obtained

Languages

List other languages you speak, if you speak more than one

Product Houses

List the product houses you have been trained by

Additional Treatments

List other treatments you're qualified to carry out. This includes training courses you completed after finishing college. For example: microblading, lash extensions, intimate waxing, laser hair removal, etc.

Booking System Software

List systems/platforms you have worked with, if any

Employment History

Start Date – End Date   Name of Work Place, Area
Position/Title
Responsibilities
- List all your responsibilities
- List all your responsibilities
- List all your responsibilities
- List all your responsibilities
- List all your responsibilities

Start Date – End Date   Name of Work Place, Area
Position/Title
Responsibilities
- List all your responsibilities
- List all your responsibilities
- List all your responsibilities
- List all your responsibilities
- List all your responsibilities

Start Date – End Date   Name of Work Place, Area
Position/Title
Responsibilities
- List all your responsibilities
- List all your responsibilities
- List all your responsibilities
- List all your responsibilities
- List all your responsibilities

Interests

List your interests or hobbies

CHAPTER THREE

Interview Masterclass

Over the years I've heard countless interview questions that interviewers have asked our candidates. You may have all the attributes and skills a company is looking for, but if you don't perform well at the interview, you won't get the job. I've met many candidates who have talked themselves out of jobs – not because they didn't want the job but because they were ill-prepared. To help you in your interview preparation, I'll share with you the most popular interview questions and answers.

Great interview questions and answers

Question one: what do you know about our company?

The answer to this question shows the interviewer whether or not you've taken the time to do your research. Make sure you know as much as you can about the company interviewing you. You want to make a good impression if this is your dream role. Your research might show what potential there is for future progression. Alternatively, your research might highlight why the company isn't a good match for you. For example, your values may not be aligned with the company's. You'll save yourself a lot of potential heartache by doing your research beforehand. Find out the answers to the following questions.

- Who started the company?

- How long have they been in existence?

- What treatments do they offer?

- What product houses do they work with?

- Have they won any awards?

- Who is their typical client?

Question two: why do you want to work for us?

The company wants to know that you've identified them as a good employer to work for and that you haven't simply sent your CV to lots of different places in the hope that someone might offer you a job. Again, to answer this question, you will need to have done your research. What attracted you to them? Is it because they are a luxury brand and you want to be part of their culture? Do you like the fact that they offer certain treatments and technologies? Are they renowned for looking after their staff and offering career progression? Think of what attracts you to the company, and why.

Question three: what are your strengths?

This is the time to blow your own trumpet – in the best possible way, of course. Think of all the things you're good at. Remember, the interviewers don't know you at all, so you'll need to tell them. Think how your family and friends would describe you. Are you someone who always goes the extra mile? Are you good at time management? Selling? If so, mention these things. If your strength is customer service and you love to exceed client expectations, highlight this fact. Are you reliable, honest, and trustworthy? You might think these are a given but I can assure you they're not. Employers want to work with people they can trust. They want to work with people who give their best and get the job done. If this sounds like you, say it. Don't assume that everyone is hard-working. Plenty of employees out there are clock watchers and will do only the minimum required of them. These types of people typically have less job satisfaction. If you work hard and go above and beyond what's expected, let the interviewers know.

Question four: what are your weaknesses?

Here, you must fess up, but again, in the most positive way. Never respond to this question by saying you cannot think of any weaknesses. Nobody is perfect. Candidates who have given this response did not get the job. Focus on a weakness that won't have a detrimental effect on the role you're applying for. Perhaps your weakness is that you're uncomfortable standing up in public and talking to a crowd. Of course, if you're applying for a job on a cruise liner, promoting the spa would be included in your role, so best to think of something else.

You can also turn a negative into a positive. For example, perhaps you're a bit of a perfectionist and tend to spend too much time focusing on the details and on getting things perfect. Another way to answer this question is to think of a weakness but show how you have improved. Perhaps you weren't great at retailing products but realised it wasn't the selling you struggled with but a lack of time at the end of the treatment. You have since learned to plan better, which has allowed you to build in time to recommend products. Or you might talk about how you were previously scared of selling products and upselling treatments but have been on several courses and now feel confident in making recommendations – and as a result, your clients have achieved much better results.

Question five: where do you see yourself five years from now?

I'm not a fan of this question, but it's popular. The most common mistake people make when they answer this is to say they want to start their own businesses. Saying you want to start your own business is a sure way of talking yourself out of a job. No employer wants to feel you're just using them as a stepping stone. They want to have a sense that you're going to grow and develop with the company. Bringing on a new employee tends to entail a substantial amount of training and cost. If interviewers believe that you're going to leave after a short time, they won't want to invest time and money in you. Choose to work in a place where you can see yourself grow, develop, and learn new skills. It should be a longer-term investment for both you and your future employer. There may be opportunities to progress into management, especially if the company has more than one branch or is thinking of opening another location.

Question six: what do you think makes our company unique?

This question is another example of why it's so important to do your homework.

Before the interview, have a look at the company's website to see what sets them apart from their competitors. The following pages will give you an insight into what makes them unique.

- Why use us?

- Our philosophy

- Our promise

- Why work with us?

Question seven: in your opinion, who is our competition and why?

You need to consider the location of the business (or locations, if they have multiple stores), the services they provide, and they category they fall into. Categories include the following:

- Hair and beauty salon

- Beauty salon

- Nail bar

- Lash bar

- Wax bar

- Day spa

- Destination spa

- Hotel spa

- Aesthetic clinic

- Medi-spa

- Skin clinic

- Male grooming

- Beauty counter

- Cruise liner

Question eight: what aspect of your current role do you enjoy the most?

This question is great as it gives you the opportunity to think about what you love doing and also what you're good at. It's an opportunity for you to decide whether the job on offer is a good fit for you. Analyse whether you love the interaction with the clients, the hands-on treatments, or the satisfaction of seeing results. Do you enjoy the operational side of the business or managing and inspiring others? Whether or not you're currently job seeking, take the time to complete this exercise occasionally to steer your career in a direction that leaves you feeling fulfilled.

Question nine: how do you see yourself progressing?

When asked this question, you have to think not only about your own progression but also about how you'll fit in and progress within the company. Consider whether you want to move into management, become more of a treatment expert, or perhaps get involved in the operational and sales side of the business. Your progression will depend on your strengths and what aspects of the business you enjoy the most. Don't worry if you haven't yet decided, especially if you're just starting out. For you, progressing might mean excelling in your current role and striving to be the best you can.

Question ten: do you have any retail experience?

Having selling experience is a distinct advantage. Whether you're selling products or promoting treatments and services, you're actively encouraging clients to buy from you. Remember, by casually mentioning to a client how relaxing the room fragrance is, for example, you're subtly recommending a product. If you're experienced in achieving and exceeding targets, mention this when the topic of sales comes up.

Question eleven: how soon can you start?

Normally, when companies start advertising their roles, they're looking for someone to start as soon as possible. If you're in a position to start immediately that's great, but don't worry if you have to give four weeks' notice. Businesses factor in that they might need to wait for the right person. For them, hiring the right fit is more important than hiring someone who can start right way.

Question twelve: give an example of how you handled a customer complaint

You don't necessarily have to talk about a complaint caused by you. The interviewer wants to see if you have experience dealing with complaints and get a sense of how you would handle them in their company. Complaints are an opportunity to improve the service. The reputation of the company is at stake when there's a complaint, and the way you deal with complaints affects client retention. When dealing with a complaint, the most important thing to do is listen. In Chapter Six, we discuss how to deal with customer complaints.

Question thirteen: why did you study beauty therapy?

The word the interviewer wants most to hear is 'passion'. You studied it because you're passionate about the industry, passionate about wanting to make a difference, passionate about helping others. The hiring manager wants to recruit someone who loves what they do and is enthusiastic. If they don't get the sense that you love what you do and are wholeheartedly committed, you're not going to be the best fit for the job.

Question fourteen: what's your favourite treatment?

Interviewers ask this question to see if you'd be a suitable candidate for the business. I often meet therapists who tell me they would love to work in a five-star hotel spa but say that massage isn't one of their favourite treatments. This would be a big concern for a hotel spa, as their most popular treatments are massage and facials. So, when you research the company, be sure to look at the treatments they offer and decide if these will fit with your skills. If waxing is your favourite treatment, it would make sense to approach a wax bar or a boutique salon where waxing is a popular treatment. At a day spa, the focus is on more relaxing treatments, so you might not get the opportunity to wax as much as you'd like to.

Question fifteen: why do you want to leave your current job?

This is one of the most common interview questions. Never bad-mouth your current or previous employer. Always keep things professional. A therapist once told me she left a job because of her boss, who had a reputation for being rude. She deducted money from therapists' wages if something went wrong or if a client complained. She also accused the therapists when products went missing from the spa. In this case, I couldn't blame the therapist for leaving. But talking about issues like this in an interview might make the interviewer think you're a troublemaker. Therefore, remain professional and keep the conversation business orientated – never make it personal. It would be much better if the therapist had told me that that there hadn't been many systems and procedures in place and that she would prefer to work in a more structured environment where staff are encouraged to do well.

Question sixteen: how would you describe yourself?

Keep it short and to the point. Think of your strengths. If you're unsure how to describe yourself, ask a friend or colleague how they would describe you and use this as a starting point. Sometimes we're a little hard on ourselves and don't see ourselves as others do.

Question seventeen: what are your salary expectations?

Don't bring up the *S* word (salary) unless prompted. If the interviewer does ask you this question, you must consider a few things before answering.

- If you know the salary on offer and it's a fixed rate that you're happy with, say that the offering is in line with what you're expecting.

- If the salary on offer is fixed but you feel you have more experience and the role warrants a higher salary, you could say you were hoping for a higher salary but for the right position you're willing to be flexible. Ask if there will be a salary review after the probation period.

- If there's a salary range, you must determine where your experience lies on the scale. If you feel you're at the higher end, you should say that with your experience, you're looking at the top end of the scale. Then, state what you can bring to the company, to strengthen your case.

- If you have no idea what the salary is, it would be best to say what you're currently earning and that you're hoping to advance your career financially.

I've seen people talk themselves out of a job because they pitch too high when the salary discussion comes up. When a company decides to offer you a role, they are taking a financial risk. They don't yet know if you are in fact as good as you say you are. Therefore, don't focus on salary alone when deciding whether or not to accept a job offer.

Question eighteen: what has been your biggest achievement to date?

This doesn't need to be a professional achievement. Choose something that stretched you as a person. Give an example of a time when you were out of your comfort zone but learned a great deal in the process and, as a result, realised that you're strong and courageous. For example, you might choose an achievement which allowed you the opportunity to make a difference in others' lives.

Question nineteen: do you have any questions?

This is often where interviews go downhill. Recently, a client told me they hadn't offered a role to a candidate because she had asked questions regarding sick pay, holiday entitlement, and days off. The client felt that the candidate was more interested in having time off than in working. These are important questions, but the timing was wrong. Ask about these things once the company has offered you the role. Also, don't feel you *have* to ask questions. The idea of the first meeting is to see if there is synergy between the two parties. If there is, you'll likely be asked back for a second interview.

Question twenty: tell us about a time you went the extra mile for a customer

Going the extra mile means doing something that isn't part of your job description, or doing something unexpected. Exceeding customers' expectations in this way creates a memorable impression. If you cannot think of an example, be sure to go that extra mile this week, so you have an example to offer during your next interview. I'll never forget what a therapist did for me once. It was such a kind and unexpected gesture that it has stayed with me for many, many years.

I had an appointment booked for a wax as soon as the salon opened, at 9.00am. I hadn't been to the salon before, and the therapist asked me if I lived nearby. I said I was a student at the university not far from the salon. She asked me if I had a class that day. I quietly said I was attending my mom's funeral later, so I wouldn't be going to class. It took all my courage not to cry. She said, 'I'm so very sorry to hear this', and continued the treatment. Neither of us spoke. When I got to the counter to pay, she asked me if I would wait for a couple of minutes. She came back and apologised for keeping me waiting but explained that she'd wanted to pop out and buy me flowers. Handing me the loveliest bunch of flowers, she said, 'I'm thinking of you.' This therapist spent her own money on me even though we'd never met before.

Question twenty-one: are you happy to work evenings and weekends?

In the beauty industry, you're probably going to have to work evenings and weekends sometimes. This tends to be the most popular time for clients. Saying that you don't want to work evenings and weekends is like saying you don't want to be in the industry. If your circumstances dictate that you cannot manage evenings and weekends, think about whether there's a different avenue within the industry that could accommodate you, as most salons, spas, hotels, and clinics want flexibility.

Question twenty-two: what are your hobbies and interests outside of work?

I love this question. It gives insight into what the person enjoys doing and how they spend their time outside of work. And it gives you the opportunity to showcase another part of yourself and sell yourself in a different way. For example, you might say, 'I love going to the gym. After a long day at work, I enjoy the feeling of doing something active, and I always feel great afterwards. I find that if I exercise, I have more energy and can cope with challenges better.'

Question twenty-three: do you have any other interviews lined up?

Be honest. If you have other interviews lined up, say so. The hiring process is a lot smoother when everyone knows where they stand. It's understandable that you would have more than one interview scheduled, as you want to choose the best opportunity for yourself. The chances are that the interviewer will be meeting other candidates too.

FACTORS TO CONSIDER BEFORE YOU ACCEPT A JOB OFFER

We spend one-third of our day, if not more, working. Consequently, it's important to work at a company where you'll be happy. Consider the following:

- Do I like the people I'll be working with?
- Will I be able to grow and develop personally and professionally?
- Can I see myself working in this environment long term?
- Is the commute reasonable and financially doable?

Seven mistakes people make during interviews

Interviews can be such a nerve-wracking experience. In a short space of time you have to showcase your skills and expertise and leave the interviewer feeling that they have found *the one*.

We recently put two candidates forward for the same role. They both received the same job spec and when I quizzed them it was clear that they both had done their research on the company. When the owner of the company interviewed them and gave me feedback, he claimed that one candidate knew very little about the company. I was surprised. The candidates later told me he did not ask them any questions about his company. The one candidate said she managed to mention that she researched the website and they ended up talking about the treatments on offer. He told her he was impressed by her knowledge. The other candidate did not create an opportunity for the interviewer to see how knowledgeable she was and unfortunately lost the role she so badly wanted.

I want to share with you some common mistakes people make at interviews and how you can avoid them, to give yourself the best chance to be considered for the job.

They don't make a good first impression

It takes seven seconds to make a first impression. If the first impression isn't great, it will take several positive experiences to change the person's perception of you. In an interview, you don't have the luxury of follow-up opportunities to impress the interviewer – so get it right from the start. This means smiling when you meet the interviewer and looking them in the eye when you shake hands. Bear in mind that the first impression starts the moment you walk through the company's door. If you're early and have to wait a few minutes for the interviewer, don't slouch or talk on your phone in the reception area. Sit up straight and think of all the great answers you have prepared.

They don't research the company

If an interviewer asks, 'What do you know about our company?' and you have nothing to say, you'll turn them off quickly. Study their website and find out everything you can about them, so you can respond in an eloquent way.

They say they want to learn

Learning and developing is fantastic, but therapists often make the mistake of telling the interviewer how much they want to learn. The focus then switches to how much they don't know. It highlights the fact that there are gaps in their education and skill set. Instead, focus on what you *do* know and what value you can add.

They don't verbalise their strengths

Have a list of strengths ready to share with the interviewer. Talk about all the things you're great at, and why they should employ you. If you come across as unsure or hesitant, the hiring manager won't feel confident about your ability to do the job.

They ask the wrong questions

This isn't so much about the questions as it is about the timing of them. Remember the candidate who asked about sick pay and holiday entitlement? Wait until someone has actually made you a job offer. These issues are irrelevant if there's no offer on the table – and asking about them can give interviewers the wrong impression of your priorities.

They come across as a smarty pants

Many therapists fall into this trap. They think asking certain questions or taking the lead in the interview will somehow give them an advantage. Recently, I spoke with a therapist who told me she had asked an interviewer about the company's future plans and where the interviewer saw herself in five years. Be mindful that the person interviewing you isn't going to share confidential or personal information. The interview isn't about them, and you can easily cause offence. Be sure to keep the focus on what you can bring to the business.

They talk about salary

A great number of people make the mistake of asking about the salary before being offered a position. Of course you'll need to know the salary and what's on offer before you can accept a position. But first, you need to convince the interviewer that you're the right person for the role. Let them come back to you with an offer, or let them bring up the salary topic themselves. Once there's an offer, the salary negotiations can start.

Tips for nailing a phone interview

Some companies prefer to conduct a phone interview first and then decide whether getting you in for a face-to-face interview is worth their while. Here are a few tips:

- Set your alarm as a reminder to call the interviewer (or to be ready for them to call you) at exactly the agreed time

- Choose a quiet place where there isn't any background noise

- Make sure you have enough battery power on your phone and a strong signal

- Smile when you talk – this might sound strange, as they cannot see you, but you'll sound a lot friendlier

- Don't interrupt the person interviewing you

- Don't use slang or swear words

- Have a glass of water on hand, in case you get a dry throat

- Try not to give yes and no answers – elaborate if you can, as this will make the conversation flow more easily.

VIDEO CALL CHECKLIST

Sit at a table or a desk.

Choose a plain background so the interviewer will focus on you instead of being distracted by things in the background.

Position your phone or laptop so it shows you at a good angle. If you're using your laptop, pop a few books underneath it so the camera doesn't look straight at you but is slightly higher than you are. Do the same thing with your phone. Position it so that you have to look up slightly at the camera.

Wear a smart top – ideally, something plain so it doesn't distract the interviewer.

Do a practice run with a friend beforehand so that you know exactly what position you'll be in when you do the real interview, and what the sound quality is like with or without your headphones.

Be mindful of your facial expressions. You want to come across as friendly and engaged.

PART TWO

MOVING FORWARD

CHAPTER FOUR

Fast Forward From Beauty Therapist To Senior Therapist

Once you have your first job as a beauty therapist, you can accelerate promotion opportunities and increase your salary if you know what employers are looking for when they recruit a senior therapist. In this chapter we discuss the things you should avoid and how to become so successful that your clients are on a waiting list to see you.

The four things you need to know to advance your career

Attitude is everything

To be a successful therapist, you need to have the right attitude. You're in charge of your attitude. You might feel that it's hard to be upbeat because life isn't great at the moment or you have a lot going on. Don't let outside circumstances drag you down. If you choose to have a positive attitude, others will want to be around you. Your clients will want to come to you for treatments, as they'll leave feeling uplifted and energised.

The next time someone asks you how you are, instead of focusing on the negatives, think of all the positives and answer with one word: 'terrific,' 'fantastic,' 'wonderful,' 'great'. Be sincere when you answer. Even if you're feeling sad, overwhelmed, or tired, you still have lots to be thankful for. A positive attitude means that you'll have more clients, and you'll make a positive impact on the atmosphere at work.

When recruiting, most managers look for people with the right attitude. You may be a talented therapist who's great at doing treatments, but if your attitude sucks, it'll have a negative impact on both your colleagues and the business as a whole.

Passion is key

Passion leads to success. Do you love what you do? You shouldn't dread going to work on Monday (I call that dread the 'Sunday feeling'). Successful people get to where they are because they really enjoy what they do. Steve Jobs said,

'If you don't love something, you're not going to go the extra mile, work the extra weekend, challenge the status quo as much.'

If you have that dreaded Sunday feeling, you have two options: change your attitude to see how you can make your work more enjoyable and meaningful or get another job. Life is too short to be unhappy. Sometimes things will feel a bit stale and you'll simply lack motivation. If this is the case, enrol in a course or do some extra training. This'll give you renewed energy and help you refocus your attention, reignite your passion, and retrieve your spark.

People like to do business with people they like

You may be a great therapist who provides results-driven treatments, but if your clients don't like you, they won't rebook with you. If your colleagues don't like you, this will affect the working environment – they want to work with someone who is a team player. The industry we're in is about building relationships with people. How you interact with others, and not how good your treatments are, determines your success. Thank clients for their custom and for choosing to have the treatment with you. Clients want to feel valued and appreciated. Thanking them helps to create client loyalty. And thanking your colleagues when they help you out creates an atmosphere of community and team spirit.

You're running a business within a business

When working as a therapist in a salon or spa, you are effectively running a business within a business. You need some business management skills to make your treatment room profitable. With every client you treat, you not only have the opportunity to make money – you also have an opportunity to make a difference in that client's life. Your primary goal is to fill the white spaces in your treatment column, to have a fully booked diary as well as clients on a waiting list, wanting to see you. You have to engage with clients to win deals (treatments), and delight them so they come back for more.

Seven mistakes therapists make in the treatment room

They ask the wrong questions

Therapists need to gain a certain amount of information from the client to provide an excellent treatment. A lot of therapists love to chat and ask questions but tend to ask the wrong questions. Focus on treatment-specific questions. Ask clients about their skincare concerns or what prompted them to come for the treatment. Don't ask questions such as 'Are you going anywhere nice on holiday?' just to fill the silence. Ask questions that will give you better insight into your clients' treatment goals so you can help them achieve these.

They don't leave the treatment room

You need to give your clients privacy to get ready for their treatments. Even your regular, seasoned clients should be given a quiet moment to prepare. There's nothing worse than a therapist being present in the room when you're undressing and getting comfortable on the bed. Always leave the room. Don't ask the client if they want you to – just politely tell them you'll be leaving to allow them time to change. Always knock on your return.

They don't explain procedures

Imagine a client is booked in for a back massage. You take them to the treatment room and let them change. When you get back, the client is lying face up on top of the towel. You're thinking, 'What's wrong with this person? Why would they lie face up on top of the towel when they're going to have a back massage?' The reason is that you didn't explain the procedure to them. Always explain what you expect them to do when you leave the room. Let them know what items of clothing they should remove or keep on, as many people will be unsure. If you want them to lie face down under the towel, say so.

They don't explain the treatment

Don't assume your client has had the treatment before. Always explain the treatment procedure.

Also, explain why you're using certain techniques or products. This will clarify the benefit of the treatment and confirm how it can help them meet their specific needs. When your clients already know the advantages of the products, and how they can be of benefit, it makes selling these products a lot easier.

They don't switch their phone off

This is one sure way to ruin your clients' treatments. It's the small things that matter, and letting your phone vibrate or ring during the treatment is unacceptable.

They don't smell good

Your treatments may be fantastic, but it's going to be tough building a loyal client base if your clients get even a whiff of body odour, stale cigarettes, or bad breath. Do whatever it takes to provide clients with an environment that is fresh and hygienic.

They don't give aftercare advice or recommend products

When you go the doctor, you expect to be given advice or recommendations. The same applies in beauty therapy. After a treatment, you cannot simply say to the client, 'I'll leave you to get ready and see you outside.' Bring each treatment to a close with advice on what your clients should or should not do. This is important – you want your clients to benefit fully from the treatment. The same goes for recommending products. You want your clients to experience the best possible result from the treatment, and for better results, they need to continue using the products.

The c word

Many beauty therapists are guilty of this mistake. Chit-chat. They talk far too much. One of the most valuable skills you can have is knowing how to really listen. It's called active listening. With active listening, you respond to information instead of leading the conversation. You gain a much better understanding of the content of the information. If you want to be a better therapist, listen more and talk less.

The average person speaks at a rate of about 125 words per minute, while the average person listens four times faster. This gives us a lot of time to think of other things and not focus on what's being said. For example, we're blocked from truly listening when we daydream, if we find the conversation boring, or if we're impatient to give our point of view. We also drift off when a word the person says leads us to an entirely different place in our minds. Sometimes the person we're speaking to will say something we disagree with, and we'll stop listening to the rest of the conversation because we're preparing our answer or argument. Quite often we get so busy with the thoughts in our heads that we don't truly hear what's being said.

When I worked in a health spa, my clients used to tell me the most intimate details of their lives. Often, I was privy to information that not even their husbands or wives knew. I remember a client telling me that she was having an affair with her husband's brother. When clients confide in you, it's important not to give advice or judge them. You want your clients to trust you. If the trust is broken, you will lose your client. As therapists, it sometimes feels as if we take on the role of a counsellor, but it's important to remember we are not trained counsellors but experts in beauty therapy.

Building a waiting list

How can you become so popular that clients are willing to go on a waiting list to see you? There's a fantastic sushi restaurant in Cape Town called Willoughby & Co. And without fail, there's always a long queue of people outside, waiting to be seated. The restaurant is close to the sea and the mountain but has no view whatsoever – it's situated in the middle of a shopping centre. But it serves the best sushi in town, and people are prepared to wait. Near the Art Institute in Chicago is a restaurant called Wildberry Pancakes and Cafe. It is described on TripAdvisor as 'worth the wait'. Near our office in Richmond, there's a restaurant called Al

Boccon di'vino. It's tiny and has no menu. You have to eat what you're given and cannot arrive at the time of your choice – you are told what time dinner starts. Yet, this place is always booked out weeks in advance. The owners create an unforgettable experience. They greet you with enthusiasm when you walk through the door, and the entire evening is memorable.

What do these restaurants do to ensure they're fully booked day after day? How can we learn from them and apply it to the beauty industry?

Successful restaurants run their businesses with efficiency. Even when they're fully booked, they look after their customers. Their aim is to ensure you have a wonderful time when you're on their premises. As a therapist, you need to run your column with the same efficiency. To do so, you need to manage your time effectively. You cannot keep clients who've booked a certain time slot to see you waiting. To be a VIP therapist, you need to run on time, every time. Often, I hear therapists say that they ran overtime because the client wanted additional treatments, or because they needed more time to get the desired results. For example, if your client doesn't have regular pedicures, you're going to be pushed for time to perform miracles with the first treatment. You can't keep the next client waiting as a result. That said, it's important not to rush treatments or to give clients the impression that you're stressed. Just as a personal trainer tells clients that they need a course of sessions to see results, you need to prescribe regular treatments to your clients.

The restaurants in Cape Town, Chicago, and London do one thing extremely well: they are consistent in what they offer. It's not hit or miss. Remarkable therapists need to be consistent in their treatments. Unless you're doing a customised treatment tailored to a client's needs, you need to provide exactly the same treatment every time. Follow the same procedure and framework and do things in the same order. Having a set structure makes it easier for you to be consistent and, ultimately, to provide your clients with the best treatment.

If you asked the man working in the sushi restaurant what was in the rainbow roll and he told you he had no idea, you wouldn't trust him. The same goes for therapies. If you aren't familiar with every treatment your salon, spa, or clinic provides, your customers aren't going to trust you. Learn your products so that you know the key ingredients and why they work. You must be able to discuss the treatments, as well as the products and their benefits, confidently. Clients are extremely treatment and product savvy. As a therapist, you instil confidence if you're knowledgeable. Make sure you know what's going on in the industry and are aware of the latest treatments and trends. Have a growth mentality and make a conscious effort to develop and learn new skills. Utilise opportunities to go on training courses.

The manager at the restaurant in Richmond greets customers like long-lost cousins when they arrive at the door. The chef pops out to see you during the meal, and if you leave food on your plate, he will cheekily ask you why. A bit extreme, but it works. He gets immediate feedback if you're unhappy with the food and has an immediate opportunity to make it better for you or to change the way he does things. He really cares and wants customers to come back. As therapists, we need to really care about our clients. There's so much competition out there – it's easy for a client to be tempted to try another therapist or to give another clinic or spa a go. When you care and are sincere in wanting to help, you will stand apart from the competition.

If a restaurant is on Trip Advisor, customers have the opportunity to encourage or discourage others from going there. Referrals are an extremely powerful tool. Is your salon, clinic, or spa on a website where customers can rate their experience? If you aren't sure, find out. You need clients to be talking about their experiences with you. For this to happen, you need to provide a remarkable service, but you also need to make sure that customers know your name. Make it easy for them to tell others about you.

Restaurants that have waiting lists also have public profiles where customers can read more about them. Start to raise your profile. When clients refer their friends to you, these friends will want to know more about you. Give them extra information about why you're the one they should choose to have the treatment with. Don't let them call up the spa and book any therapist. Start raising your profile and you'll see your treatment column start to fill up.

When you go to a restaurant, the staff always tells you about the specials. Although the restaurant might be known for its sushi or steak, they still want you to know what else is delicious. As a therapist, you might have a regular client who comes to you for facials. You need to introduce this person to other treatments that you think will benefit them. You might take it for granted that your clients know what treatments are on the menu or what products your salon, spa, or clinic provides. Do not assume. Tell them about the latest treatments, innovations, and products that may benefit them. It's much easier to sell to an existing client who knows and trusts you than to a complete stranger.

Restaurants are great at leaving you with their business card when you pay the bill. Likewise, therapists should get into the habit of not just leaving the client with their name but also suggest booking their next appointment, so they get their preferred day and time slot. If you're not doing this already, make it a priority.

A wonderful saying by Maya Angelou sums up how to treat customers to ensure you build up a strong and loyal customer base:

> 'People will forget what you said, people will forget what you did, but people will never forget how you made them feel.'

CHAPTER FIVE

How To Go From Beauty To Aesthetics

It isn't always easy to make the switch from beauty therapy to aesthetics, especially if you've been working in spas where the focus is on massage and hands-on facials.

Some companies provide training, but a large percentage of businesses prefer candidates to already have some experience in providing advanced treatments. You will be more of an asset to a business if you can provide treatments straight away and don't need to attend a host of training courses before you start generating money.

Different aesthetic environments

Within aesthetics there are different environments, some of which are easier to get into than others.

Beauty salons with IPL/laser treatments

This is the easiest route into aesthetics. If you already provide most of the face and body treatments the company offers, you would just need to up-skill in laser and IPL (intense pulsed light) hair removal and skin rejuvenation. You might also have the opportunity to learn other advanced treatments such as LED phototherapy, microneedling, and skin tightening.

Medi-spas

Medi-spas offer traditional beauty and holistic treatments, plus advanced treatments under the supervision of a doctor. It's likely that the company would start you off doing traditional face and body treatments. After your probation period, they would send you on advanced training courses to learn other procedures, e.g. cryolipolysis (fat freezing), IPL/laser hair removal, skin resurfacing, tattoo removal, ultrasound, skin tightening treatments and various peels. Medi-spas offer clients a comprehensive list of holistic, beauty, and aesthetic treatments – all under one roof. Working in a medi-spa is a good option if you want to exercise your skills as a beauty therapist while training to become an aesthetic therapist/ technician.

Aesthetic clinics

Aesthetic clinics offer no beauty or holistic therapies. The focus is purely on advanced face and body treatments. The treatment menu may include dermal fillers, anti-wrinkle injections, PRP therapy and mesotherapy. Aesthetic therapists concentrate on skin rejuvenation treating acne, pigmentation, vascular lesions and scarring. Other services might include chemical peels, laser treatments, body sculpting, skin tightening and cellulite reduction.

Skin clinics

These clinics concentrate on skin health. Typically, they focus on facial treatments. Several high-tech machines are used to give clients who want blemish-free, younger-looking skin the best results. In skin clinics, therapists are called aesthetic facialists, skin therapists, or dermal therapists. Facials are at the core of the treatment menu, and clients benefit from treatments such as IPL for skin rejuvenation, LED phototherapy, microneedling, skin peels, radio frequency and laser resurfacing. If you're passionate about skin, this is a good option.

ARE YOU SUITABLE FOR AESTHETICS?

Use this checklist to see whether an aesthetic environment would suit you.

- Do you have extensive skincare knowledge?
- Are you personable? Someone who can instil confidence in clients?
- Do you have retail experience and a proven record of selling treatments and recommending products for home care?
- Do you present yourself impeccably?
- Do you have experience providing advanced treatments and do you hold the certificates and diplomas as backup?
- Do you offer high levels of customer care?
- Are you a great communicator who is able to manage client expectations?
- Are you flexible and able to work evenings and weekends?
- Are you consistent in achieving targets?
- Are you organised and meticulous in keeping patient notes and consent forms?

Progression roles

Working within aesthetics can be incredibly rewarding, as you can help restore people's confidence and boost their self-esteem. From hands-on aesthetics, the most popular next step is to become a registered clinic manager. In this role, you have the opportunity to lead teams and drive sales. You need to be confident in dealing with complaints and in motivating teams to achieve their targets. Clinic managers must have a positive attitude, to inspire their teams. A flair for sales and working to targets is essential. A substantial amount of administration is involved in this role, so you need to be organised and focused. It's imperative to have a thorough understanding of treatment procedures and trends.

Another popular step up from hands-on aesthetics is to work as a trainer for an aesthetic brand. Trainers need patience, empathy, a positive attitude, and enthusiasm. Inspiring others requires you to have in-depth knowledge of products and procedures. The success of your students will be your primary goal.

If you're a natural seller, working as a sales representative for an aesthetic brand would suit you. Typically, sales reps are in charge of a region and their main responsibilities are business development and managing relationships with stockists. Being a sales rep involves travelling, so if you prefer to be based in one place, this role isn't for you.

Training

If you think aesthetics is for you, the first step is a conversation with your current manager to see if there's an opportunity to train in advanced treatments.

It's easier to develop your skills with your current employer than to apply for aesthetic roles with no advanced treatment experience.

In the UK, a level 3 diploma with electrical equipment training is essential. Most aesthetic clinics require you to have a level 4 qualification. If you reside outside the UK, check the licencing requirements.

Some colleges are affiliated with dermatology practices, recruitment agencies, and cosmetic clinics, and will recommend you to companies at the end of your training. This can help you secure an aesthetics role with greater ease.

CHAPTER SIX

Management Crash Course

Often we are thrown into the deep end when it comes to managing others. Sometimes we feel we have not had adequate training to deal with the trials and tribulations of motivating and inspiring others to achieve success. This chapter will guide you and help you bring out the best in your team, build the business and create customer loyalty.

How to get into management

If you don't have the title yet, here are fifteen ways to speed up the process and get you closer to becoming a manager.

Step up

You need to excel in your current role. Think of what you can do today that will make you stand out from your peers. Getting to the next level isn't about being mediocre and doing what everyone else is doing. It's about stepping up. What responsibilities can you take on in addition to providing treatments? We often advertise managerial roles. Many beauty therapists apply, but their CVs show no management responsibilities. To be considered for such a role, applicants need to have undertaken additional responsibilities, apart from doing treatments.

Take on more tasks

Write down your current responsibilities and what you do on a day-to-day basis at work. Then write down what you think your boss or manager does. Now compare the lists. This will help you to see the gaps in your own list and what tasks you need to learn or take on in order to move into management.

Assist your current manager

Learn on the job. Don't wait for your manager to give you tasks. Be proactive. Ask what you can do. Or, use your initiative and do something that will benefit the company. Your job will become more meaningful if you take on extra tasks or help others. It's when you step out of your comfort zone that you grow and develop.

Doing something for the first time can be daunting, but the more you do it, the more comfortable you will become with it.

Do things that are *not* in your job description

If you're serious about getting into management then start doing tasks that aren't in your job description. Your job description outlines the general duties and expectations your company has of you – this is for the average employee to carry out their role.

Getting into management and being a leader is about doing what others aren't prepared to do. Often this means getting your hands dirty – literally. I've worked in places that require the therapists to clean their treatment rooms with a toothbrush to get into the nooks and crannies. Some of the therapists complain and say they weren't hired to be cleaners, but the beauty industry isn't all glamour. Behind the scenes you pick up dirty towels, do laundry, and clean the floor.

Have a positive attitude

Without a positive attitude, forget about getting into management. If you want to be an inspiring leader, attitude is key. You choose your attitude. It's not dictated by circumstances.

One of our candidates demonstrated exactly this when we sent her to an interview at a high-profile clinic in London. She had just paid a landlord a hefty deposit for a flat and was due to move later that day. On the way to the interview, she found out that the landlord was a con artist and had run off with the money. There was no flat. It was all a scam. Instead of letting this affect her interview, she made a choice to stay positive and calm. She didn't mention the incident at her interview. This proved that she could separate her private life from her work life.

Showing up and deciding to be happy and positive is a choice, regardless of what happens at home. When you have a positive attitude at work, it makes you more productive – and it makes the work environment more fun.

Be flexible and adapt

Gearing yourself up for management means you need to learn to be flexible and able to adapt to change. Recently, during an interview, I asked a candidate why she wanted to leave her current role. She told me the job had turned out differently from the way she'd imagined it. My guess was she would find herself in a similar position in her next role. Why? Because circumstances change, technology changes, and businesses need to adapt to survive – and so do their employees. You need to be flexible and able to roll with the punches. That's pretty much how it goes in life as well.

Years ago, while I was working at a health club as the health and beauty manager, the food and beverage manager resigned. I was asked if I would step in and look after the bar and restaurant. The great thing about taking on this role was that I learned so much. Going from beauty products that had a long shelf life to food stock rotation was very different. I was taking a big step up, from designing beauty treatment menus to planning the menus for a restaurant and overseeing a kitchen. The flexibility and desire to learn paid off, as I was asked to be the acting general manager for the club shortly after this. This experience shaped my career; it was instrumental in paving my way into upper management.

Be motivated

Managers set the tone in the business and staff productivity and engagement will be a direct result of how management motivate their teams to achieve goals. To motivate and inspire others, you need to be self-motivated. Set yourself daily targets for upselling treatments and products to keep yourself focused.

Take responsibility

When you're a manager, the buck stops with you. If things go wrong, you have to take action. You're accountable for the success of your team. So many staff members blame others when things go wrong. Instead, take responsibility for your actions. If you've messed up, admit it. If you forgot to do something, say so. Be honest. If you haven't reached your sales targets, don't blame circumstances. Instead, make a pact with yourself to work harder to reach them next time. Managers want staff members who are honest, have integrity, and take responsibility.

Use your common sense

As a manager you will have to deal with challenges on a daily basis; at times you might feel completely out of your comfort zone. When in doubt on how to handle a situation, put yourself in the shoes of the customer and think about how they would like to be treated. If faced with a crisis, think of possible solutions to the problem. Reflect on the best possible outcome and what you can do to move closer to this outcome.

Improve your social skills

Strong social skills are a key asset for managers, having empathy for others and being able to communicate effectively. Dealing with customers and knowing how to build rapport is a major part of your role; not only are social skills essential for client retention but you must hone these skills to manage your staff and bring out the best in them.

Lead by example

Take pride in your work. It's often the small details that get noticed and set you apart from others. People tend to remember the small details as the rest they take for granted. So ensure you set an example. Treat both clients and team members with respect. This includes not gossiping about others and being professional at all times.

Be punctual

If you want to be a manager, you need to be punctual to set the standard for the rest of the team. Always arrive on time and be sure to manage your time at work efficiently. Try to be early, so you're ready to go when your shift starts. There's nothing worse than a client already waiting for their treatment when a therapist walks through the door.

Be reliable

Show up no matter what. Make sure you're someone people can count on to get the job done – reliability is a fundamental quality of aspiring managers. Become someone your line manager and colleagues can trust in your commitment to complete tasks and take on managerial responsibilities.

Be honest

Relationships are built on trust. As mentioned, bosses want staff who are honest. Don't be scared to admit if you don't know how to do something. Seek guidance and build your knowledge. It's much better to be transparent than to pretend you know something and make mistakes.

Go the extra mile

The quickest way to management is to go the extra mile, by putting in great effort consistently and taking on tasks that may not be in your job description if required. The employees who stand out and make a difference are the ones who exceed expectations. These are the employees that get noticed and get promoted.

The three components of management

As manager, you will focus on three things: your team, the business, and your customers.

Your team

A good manager is someone who can lead a team – someone who can inspire, motivate, and drive people to achieve goals. Think of the best and the worst managers you've had. What qualities did they have or lack? We all have our own management styles, so find a way to bring out the best in people while remaining true to yourself.

Team checklist

- Be transparent from day one, starting with the hiring process. If you misrepresent a role, the team member will have unrealistic expectations and may not stay. I hear of people handing in their notice after learning that the working hours or commission structure at a company is different from what was pitched to them during the interview.

- Make sure you thoroughly orient all new staff members when they start. This is a make-or-break activity and will set the tone for their employment with the company. At the first spa where I worked, all new staff members were treated like guests on their first day. They were invited to have a treatment and to use the facilities. This was a wonderful introduction to the company, its people, and its processes.

- Set clear objectives so team members know exactly what is expected of them. If you aren't clear, staff will either use their own initiative or won't do anything at all.

- Ensure that the commission structure is easy to understand. When staff don't quite understand how the structure works, they become demotivated to sell.

- Have processes and systems in place and make sure that you document them. Ensure all staff members receive comprehensive training in the use of the systems and procedures. If you start working somewhere and there are no clear guidelines as to how things are done, make creating them one of your priorities. A successful business is consistent in its delivery. And consistency requires clear guidelines on how staff should execute tasks. McDonald's is a good example. The whole business is systemised, so whether you order a Big Mac in London or one in Cape Town, you'll get exactly the same item. Staff across the globe follow exactly the same procedures to deliver consistent results and please their customers.

- Hold brief daily meetings to make sure that staff are informed of daily activities, promotions, and offers.

- Have weekly staff meetings and focus on areas that could use improvement, but also celebrate the small wins. Communication is key when dealing with people. Don't let problems fester.

- Review staff training and performance every six months to maximise staff development and make everyone feel valued.

The business

As manager, you're responsible for bringing money into the business. You're in the business of selling. You have to think of ways to attract new clients to the business and to retain the clients you have. Your goal is to deliver treatments and experiences that people want to buy repeatedly. Keep in mind that there are other ways to generate money for the business besides selling treatments and products. Identify which ones would work best to boost profits and complement what you offer.

Business checklist

- Analyse each team member's monthly revenue and discuss strategies for increasing these figures.

- Identify which team members need to increase their room occupancy. Use this data to pinpoint areas of weakness or training needs.

- Establish which days and times are quiet in the salon or spa and create promotions around these for people whose time is flexible. Adapt the rota to meet seasonal needs thus ensuring maximum room occupancy and revenue.

- Determine the top-selling treatments and adjust the treatment menu accordingly. Focus on treatments that are popular and financially rewarding. Consider streamlining the treatment menu. Make it easy for clients to choose and then include add-ons to customise the treatments. This will ultimately deliver better results for both the clients and the business.

- Focus on client reviews. These play an integral part in client retention and in encouraging potential customers to book a treatment. We live in a time where customer ratings can make or break a business. Five-star reviews accelerate the success of the business, while negative reviews damage the business' reputation and kill revenue.

- Seek partnerships with local businesses: give their staff a special rate. Thriving businesses create a culture of community – people want to be part of something. Make your salon or clinic a place where people want to hang out and spend time.

- When the salon or clinic is closed or quiet, consider renting out treatment rooms to other industry professionals whose treatments will complement yours. A fixed daily or monthly rate is easier to manage than taking a percentage of their income. This ancillary income really boosts profits as the cost to the business is very low and the infrastructure is already in place.

- Get the company website set up as an e-commerce site so you can sell gift vouchers and products online. Make it easy for people to buy presents for family, friends, and loved ones.

- Have a website presence on other industry platforms to maximise exposure.

- Consider other services that could be booked and sold online, e.g. a masterclass, makeover, bridal package, spa day, or pamper party.

- Think of ways to generate recurring income.

Your customers

Customers are at the heart of your business. Without them, there is no business. Jim Rohn sums it up perfectly: 'One customer well taken care of could be more valuable than $10,000 worth of advertising.'

Customer checklist

- Invest in great staff – you need great staff to provide great customer service. When you train your staff, instil a mind-set of providing five-star service, where nothing is too much trouble.

- Map out and document the customer journey with your team. You want clients to have the same amazing experience each time they visit.

- Create a system through which customers can provide you with feedback about their treatments. This feedback is extremely valuable to keep standards high and to ensure that you can provide customers with what they need.

- At the time of booking, be sure to ask the client if the treatment is for a special occasion. Customer loyalty is all about the small touches. Gestures such as acknowledging a birthday or anticipating their needs are the things clients remember the most.

- Create a welcoming environment for clients by ensuring staff greet every customer they see in the salon, spa, or clinic, not just their own clients. And make sure that your team runs on time. Keeping clients waiting has a negative impact on their experience as well as on the business.

- Set yourself apart from other businesses providing the same treatments by paying attention to detail and personalising the customer experience.

How to deal with customer complaints

As manager, you have to be prepared to deal with complaints. Having a structure will make it easier for you to do so.

The complaining customer provides an opportunity to improve things. How you handle a complaint is crucial – you want to protect your company's reputation and also retain the client. Always bear reputation and retention in mind when dealing with complaints.

1. Listen

This is the most important step. You need to give the client the opportunity to talk. Listen and do not interrupt them. Any interruption will make the client even more frustrated and agitated.

2. Acknowledge

You need to thank the customer for bringing the problem to your attention. Don't patronise them. Now is the chance to ask questions and repeat the issue to the client. You want to make sure you understand the full extent of their complaint. The client should also feel confident that you understand the situation. Compassion and empathy will help defuse any tension and show the client that you genuinely want to help them.

3. Apologise

Say that you're sorry that this has happened. It might not be your fault, but you are representing the company, so it's important that you let the client know that you're going to do all you can to put things right. In severe cases, it might not be legally advisable to apologise, but you can still offer the client empathy by saying you're sorry that the situation has happened.

4. Offer a solution

What you're aiming for is a solution that will satisfy the customer and make them come back in future. Ask yourself, 'What does the customer want?' You may need to offer some kind of financial compensation or a discount on a future purchase, or you may simply need to apologise and reassure them that it won't happen again. The cost of satisfying the customer will most likely be less than the cost of losing the customer.

Research has shown that customers prefer the person with whom they are speaking to solve the problem and don't like being passed on to various people. If you don't have the authority to make certain decisions, tell the client that you will need to speak with the person who can help them best but that you will let them know when they can expect a response. Clients want their complaints dealt with quickly, so don't delay. This makes the situation worse.

Learn from customer complaints and use the opportunity to make things better in the future. There may be many customers who had the same experience but didn't complain. If you don't improve the situation, they will go elsewhere. Listen to what your customers are saying when they complain – they'll provide you with exact guidelines and insight into what services or products aren't up to standard.

Six things you need to teach your team

As manager you want your team to provide such a fantastic service that your clients return time and time again. In order to attract and retain clients, your team needs to provide an exceptional customer journey. The journey comprises key elements every team member should know:

1. How to get results

Your team members need to know that clients come to them for results. To provide the best results, they need to identify the problem, so ensure that each staff member carries out thorough consultations. Clients might not always say outright what their concerns are, so the staff need to find out by gently probing and questioning why they're at the salon, spa, or clinic. Once the therapists understand the clients' concerns, they can recommend the most appropriate treatments for the best results.

2. How to read body language

Teach staff to focus on body language and look out for clients' non-verbal communication. When a client flinches during a massage, they're uncomfortable – the pressure might be too intense. If they curl their toes during a waxing treatment, they're likely finding it painful. A client making a nervous movement during a manicure while the therapist is pushing the cuticles back means it's hurting. Therapists need to reassure clients, so they feel they're in good hands and that everything will be okay. Don't underestimate body language and the clues it provides. Encourage your staff to use these clues to their advantage so they can provide a better treatment.

3. How to be consistent

Clients want consistency. When they book a treatment at the salon, spa, or clinic, they want to know that they'll get great service and a treatment of the highest standard. It cannot be hit or miss. This is a sure way to not get repeat business – clients don't want to take risks. It's the manager's responsibility to ensure that the team is consistent and follows the same protocols and procedures during every treatment.

4. How to provide value for money

Clients want value for money and good service. Value for money doesn't mean cheap. It means not ripping clients off. Value is more important than cost. Teach staff to be mindful of this while doing treatments. Make sure that they know not to cut their treatments short (unless the client arrives late and they have to tailor the treatment to the time available). Also make sure that staff know exactly what each treatment entails so they don't miss steps and leave clients feeling short changed.

5. Shhhhhh – how to be quiet

Clients often want therapists to be quiet during their treatments. Teach your staff to take the cue from the client. It's important that they learn to pick up subtle hints from their customers. If the client is talkative and asks a lot of questions, then of course the therapist needs to be responsive. But if the client gives one-word answers and doesn't ask any questions, the therapist should stop talking. They don't need to fill the silence with chatter. Often, the hour-long treatment is the only 'me time' a client will have during the day. Personally, I get irritated when a therapist tries to make conversation during my massage. I want the therapist to check for contraindications and to determine what pressure I like and what areas to concentrate on, but apart from that, I want to relax and enjoy the treatment in silence.

6. How to create a lifetime client

Teach your team members how to create lifetime clients – those clients who keep on coming back again and again. How do we get them to come back? The therapist has to spend enough time during the consultation to determine what the client's face and body goals are, and the time frame in which they want to achieve them. They might have a special event coming up that they need to look their best for. The therapist can tailor-make a treatment plan that will ensure the best results. A lifetime client comes to trust the therapist who remains with them throughout the long haul of helping them look and feel their best.

CHAPTER SEVEN

Help, I Suck At Sales

Most therapists I meet tell me they aren't great at sales, yet I know this isn't true. They recommend products and services to their friends every day. For example, say someone compliments you on what you're wearing. Instead of just saying 'thank you', you tell them where you bought it. You might even tell them the price if it was a bargain. You're selling without even realising it. Or maybe you've just been to a great restaurant and tell your friends that they simply have to go and which dish they should have.

In the workplace, the same mind-set must be adopted. Many therapists shy away from sales as they think they'll ruin the treatment for the client. Think of it this way; you're not feeling great, so you book an appointment to see the doctor. The doctor does an in-depth consultation and at the end tells you it was lovely to see you and sends you on your way. This is unthinkable. You expect the doctor to provide a solution and a remedy. Similarly, if a client comes to see you because they have a certain problem, they expect you to fix it. Realistically, this might not happen over one treatment. Therefore, as the expert, it's your responsibility to recommend products for home use, as well as additional or alternative treatments to achieve the desired results.

Great salespeople know their products inside out and recommend the products or treatments that will suit their clients' needs. They never sell something just for the sake of it. There's nothing more off-putting than a pushy salesperson. Have you ever had an experience with a salesperson who was so full on that you didn't buy from them? Nobody wants to buy from people like that. If you sell this way, clients won't return.

When it comes to sales, the most important thing is to listen. Listen to what the client wants and what they're hoping to achieve. The customer has to dominate the conversation, not the therapist. Sales is about confidence. The therapist must be confident in their products and the client must feel confident in their therapist.

People don't just buy because they need something. People buy because they want something. They buy what others buy and not what others have to sell. Appeal is the strongest buying motive there is. If someone really wants something, they justify the cost to themselves or their partners and friends. We've all been there – we want something, but we don't need it. Buying a new product or treatment creates hope and excitement. Think of buying a product such as foundation. It comes with the promise that it will smooth and hydrate your skin and provide a flawless finish. When I buy an exfoliator, I buy it hoping that it will brighten my skin and even out my complexion. I buy it because I dream of having perfect skin. The driving force in buying here is emotion.

Buyers might think they've made the decision based on rational thinking, but the decision has been based on the 'I like it' principle. Customers buy because they want results. It's your job to find out what they want. If you're not sure, there's only one way to find out: ask them.

Nine strategies to help you improve your sales

The more you sell, the easier it gets. Implement the strategies and suggestions in this section when you next have the opportunity. You will immediately see the difference as you will become more confident and your sales will increase.

Be unique

Be yourself. Don't try to copy someone else. We all have our own ways of speaking, and customers want to buy from someone who's genuine – not someone who's putting on a show. In your own words, say what the products or treatments will accomplish. It's not so important to speak about the technical bits. They're there for the clients who want to know about them. Think about how Nike sells trainers. Do they give you all the technical specifications? No, their advertising campaigns show successful sports stars wearing their shoes. Nike's campaigns make consumers want to be part of the club – to be part of the success of high performance.

Ask questions

The more information you have about the customer, the easier it is to sell to them. Always provide a thorough consultation to find out what the client's concerns are and what they would like to achieve. If they're coming to you for skin-rejuvenating treatments, ask what else they're doing to reach their skin goals. Find out where the gaps are. This way, you'll be able to recommend products, supplements, or additional treatments to deliver maximum results.

Identify your ideal customer

You need to make sure you're selling to the right people. There will always be customers after freebies – those clients who just want a sample but have no intention of spending any money. That's fine. You need to identify the clients interested in buying your products. It's important to realise that the products you sell don't interest everyone. That's the nature of the business. Focus on the small percentage of people who want to buy, and delight them. When you run a marketing campaign, you'll get some clients who are after a cheap deal and who have no real interest in becoming regular clients. They are not your ideal clients. You're better off charging the full price to clients who value what you do and will come back to you, time and time again.

Determine the problem and the solution

Few people wander into a salon, clinic, or spa because they have nothing better to do. Something has enticed them to book a treatment. Find out what's brought them in and go from there.

What if you have the perfect solution for a customer but they still don't buy? Sometimes it's just about timing. For example, imagine you meet someone who tells you they're a wedding planner. You don't take much notice, as you're not planning a wedding. But a year down the line, your partner proposes to you, and suddenly you remember the wedding planner who made a great impression on you. You decide to give her a call. Always make a good impression on your clients so that even if they don't buy from you today, you'll be the first person they buy from when they're ready (or they'll recommend you to their friends).

Focus on the experience

We all like to buy, but we don't like to be sold to. Make the buying experience an enjoyable one for the client. I was in a store recently looking at lipsticks. The assistant came over and recommended a lipstick that she said was super hydrating and plumping and that she thought would go well with my skin tone. She asked me if I normally chose bright colours or if I preferred subtler shades. It opened up a conversation, and before long I was sitting down and she was applying the lipstick. It looked good, and she said it would look even better if I teamed it with the right shade of lip liner. I didn't need either, but I bought both. The product packages were tiny, but she went the extra mile by spraying tissue paper with perfume and popping it into a bag along with the products. Then she tied the bag with a ribbon. The experience would have been very different if the assistant had simply said, 'Let me know if you need anything.' I probably would have looked at the lipsticks and then walked out without buying anything.

Believe

Believing in your products and treatments will make selling them a lot easier. I remember working at a spa where there was one product that didn't shift. It was a hair mask. None of the treatments on offer incorporated this product, so it was really hard to sell. Determined to find a way to sell it, I decided to try it myself. I cannot tell you the difference doing this made to my sales. My hair was like silk, and I recommended the product to everyone I met – clients coming back from holiday who had dry and damaged hair, clients going on holiday who wanted to look their best, clients who had a special occasion coming up, and clients who felt they needed a bit of a boost because their hair was limp. It didn't feel like selling, as I was simply telling clients how amazing the mask had made my hair feel. If you're struggling with selling products, try them yourself. If they work for you, you'll speak from the heart and it will make all the difference.

Never assume

Always presume people can afford products – never assume they can't. Don't judge. Treat everyone the same way, unless they tell you they cannot afford it.

Don't be a one-hit wonder

If you want to deliver the best results to your clients, it will probably take more than one treatment, and more than one product. Treatments are a bit like exercise. One session is going to make you feel good, but you need to continue and maintain the pace if you want to see a difference. Recommend the treatments and products that will give your clients results. If money is a concern, help them decide which products or treatments to opt for first, and which ones to consider further down the line. Let clients know how to use the products economically so there's no waste.

Provide excellent customer service

Our products and treatments may be phenomenal, but if our customer service is subpar, clients aren't going to come back. Customer service is what sets us apart from the competition. The next time you meet a client, think of the customer journey you're providing. Think of ways you can improve it and make every client feel like a million dollars, every step of the way.

Thanks, but no thanks

For sales to happen, we need a yes. If people turn you down when you propose a product or a treatment, it means there's something missing.

- **There's no need for your offer**

  Rewind to when you did your consultation with the client. Based on this consultation, they may not feel a need for the product you're currently recommending. Reflect on whether you fully understand their concerns and have explained the benefits and effects of the product.

- **You haven't created urgency**

  Clients might love the product but not feel a need for it straight away. In this case, you need to work on improving the language you use so that it creates excitement and entices clients to take action immediately and start seeing results.

- **There's no desire for your product**

  Successful brands create desire for their products. People feel they simply have to have them. Again, when selling products or treatments, you need to create a feeling of excitement by using enticing language.

- **There's no trust**

  Clients buy from people they trust. Trust takes time to build, so be patient. Clients will trust you if they feel you're an authority, so make sure you know your product ingredients and their benefits. The same goes for treatments. Try to experience for yourself the treatments your company offers so you can talk first-hand about what the client can expect. Providing your clients with sample products will give them the opportunity to try them before they buy them.

- **There's a money issue**

  If you have proved yourself as an authority but clients are turning down your offer because of a lack of money, they will buy from you when the time is right.

Remember that the best salespeople are the ones who are great listeners, as they get to know exactly what the client wants.

PART THREE

BLAZING A TRAIL

CHAPTER EIGHT

Hands-Off Career Options

Many therapists tell me that they love the industry but don't want to be hands-on any more. Fortunately, there are so many opportunities for therapists in this industry. Whether it's front of house, sales, or administration that interests you, it's important to find the role that suits you best.

Beauty blogger

Utilising your love and knowledge of all things beauty and turning it into a paid job requires strategy, dedication, and passion. I asked an expert blogger how to turn your hobby into your career by blogging. I first met Collette Stohler in Bali, and she was already living the dream life. Collette co-founded an award-winning travel blog called *Roamaroo*, and the brand has gained cult status. I wanted to learn what it takes to be a blogger and influencer – what happens behind the scenes to make it happen.

I asked Collette about how to make the transition from permanent job to full-time blogger. She said that as a beauty therapist, you're the expert in your field and there's great value in that. If you want to transition from an in-spa therapist to a blogger, the best thing to do is to start writing. She advocates sharing your love of beauty with the world and says there's no better time than the present. Collette went on to say that blogging isn't as simple as one might think. To be successful as a blogger, you need to wear many hats: entrepreneur, search engine optimisation (SEO) specialist, photographer, writer, editor, and web designer.

Collette advises that before you create your website, you need to think about your unique selling point and your specialities. Do you specialise in anti-ageing treatments? Have you created a secret serum that no one knows about? Collette recommends that, in an age where everyone wants to be a blogger, first figure out what makes you and your brand special, and then craft your writing from there. She says that blogging is a community and recommends reaching out to beauty bloggers who have inspired you – ask if you can start writing for them. She explains that by writing articles for other people, you capitalise on their 'link juice' and begin to develop relationships. She recommends signing up for HARO (Help a Reporter Out). HARO is a fantastic way to be featured as a beauty expert in various news outlets.

When I asked Collette what she knows now and wished she'd known when she started out, she said she wished she'd studied SEO before developing her blog. She has a writing background and believed that if she wrote, they would come. But because she wasn't using the right key words, it didn't matter that her articles were top-notch and informative – no one could find them. She recommends using a service like Google AdWords to see what people are searching for before writing an article.

Collette also talked about how important it is to collaborate with other companies and brands. She explained that because blogging is a community, it's important to develop relationships with other bloggers as well as other brands. She mentioned that there are many blogger communities on Facebook which can be extremely helpful in your blogging journey.

I was curious about how easy it is to make money from blogging, and what strategies would accelerate success. Collette explained that blogging isn't an easy job if you want to make money. As a travel blogger, she constantly gets asked 'How do I get paid to travel?' She explained that, as you do in any job, you have to offer a service and value in order to make a living. First and foremost, you have to bring passion and unrelenting grit to the table. Collette said blogging isn't an easy career path, but if you stay true to your passion, it's worth it.

She pointed out that there are a multitude of ways to make money as a blogger. One option is to *sell advertising* on your website. She went on to say that you could charge according to the number of unique monthly views and the demographics of your viewers. Automated services, such as Google Ads, integrate advertisements on your website. Another way to make money as a blogger is through *affiliate marketing*. With affiliate marketing, you make money based on the number of people who click through and/or buy products linked to your website. Two affiliate marketing services Collette recommends are Rakuten Marketing and Commission Junction.

Yet another way to make money is by *selling sponsored posts and product reviews* on your website. Collette said that the tricky part about this is that if you accept money in exchange for writing about a product, any link to the product will have a 'no-follow' link, meaning that the search engines cannot influence the link's ranking in a search engine index.

COLLETTE'S TOP-THREE TIPS FOR AN ASPIRING BLOGGER

1. Be willing to work for free in the beginning. Reach out to people who inspire you and ask if you can shadow them or write for them for free (and politely ask for a link in return). Practise

your writing, hone your skills, and discover your unique voice. Of course, you should do all of this while developing your own blog. You'll earn the respect of your peers, prove your value, and develop your brand, all in one go.

2. Be gritty. You have to have passion behind your purpose to make blogging a full-time job. There will be times when you hit a wall, or you may be told by others that you can't do something, but if you're willing to put your head down and persevere, nothing can stop you.

3. Adapt. Blogging and digital marketing change daily. The rules are constantly being rewritten. Sign up for newsletters, such as **SmartBrief**, and read leading trade magazines and the newspaper to gain an understanding of current events and changes in the digital world. As algorithms and rules change, you must educate yourself and be willing to adapt in order to succeed.

Front of house/clinic coordinator

Being the first point of contact in a clinic or spa is an important role. To succeed at the front desk, you need to have the following qualities:

Organisational skills. The front desk requires someone who can multitask. It may be that the phones are ringing, a client walks in, and someone is at the

113

desk wanting to pay for their treatment all at the same time. The trick is to start the day with everything in place and to stay on top of things as you go along.

Calm under pressure. You must be like the gracious swan – beneath the surface you're paddling like crazy, but above the water you're cool, calm, and collected. Despite what may be happening behind the scenes, you need to create a calm environment where clients feel relaxed and nurtured. I once helped out at a clinic where the doctor constantly ran late. This had a knock-on effect on the appointments. My challenge was to keep the clients happy in spite of the wait.

Excellent timekeeper. As the front of house person, you'll often be asked to open or close the premises. This means that you need to be punctual. If starting early or finishing late doesn't suit your lifestyle, most front of house roles won't suit you.

Exceptional telephone manner. On the telephone, you need to be friendly and efficient. One of the clinics we work with has an exceptional receptionist. I have never, ever caught her off guard. She always sounds happy and upbeat. I know the clinic gets super busy, and she's often trying to do 101 things at once, but when she picks up the phone, she always sounds genuinely pleased to hear from me. And she adopts this tone with every single caller.

Know your stuff. When booking appointments, you need to fully understand each treatment on the menu.

Clients may want information and reassurance if they haven't had the treatment before. Ensure that you know what happens during the treatment and which clients it would suit. It's costly and embarrassing if a client is booked for a treatment only to be told by the therapist they aren't suitable for the treatment when they arrive. If the client needs to do any prep before they come in, you need to mention this too. For example, if they're having a spray tan, remind them to exfoliate beforehand and to wear loose, dark clothing. If a client is having a treatment that requires downtime afterwards, remind them of this so that they don't plan to go out afterwards.

Comfortable with the S word. A good front of house person is great with sales. But not in a pushy way. You're responsible for getting the white spaces – the gaps in the treatment diary – filled up. This means knowing who's booked on a course of treatment so you can rebook them within the correct time frame. A good front of house person always makes sure that clients or patients are aware of any new treatments available at the clinic and of open evenings and demonstrations (see also Chapter Seven).

Seven front desk mistakes and how to avoid them

Mistake one: not analysing the bookings

At the start of your shift, be sure to analyse the treatment columns to familiarise yourself with who's coming in and what treatments they're having. Are they coming in pairs or as part of a group? Has the treatment been booked as a birthday present or to celebrate an anniversary? You want to give each client a warm welcome. The busier the day, the more important it is to be prepared, so that things run smoothly.

Mistake two: losing walk-in business

Often, therapists aren't trained to deal with walk-in customers and end up losing both current and future business because they fail to make a good first impression. The first objective when someone walks into your salon, spa, or clinic is to make them feel welcome by greeting them. The second is to establish what treatment they would like. If you have availability, get them booked in. If you have additional time, suggest add-on treatments. If you need to juggle the schedule a little, ask them to take a seat and offer them refreshments while they wait. Explain that you're going to see if you can accommodate them. If there's no availability, offer alternative dates. Whether they accept or decline, give them a treatment brochure to take away and politely ask them to book in advance whenever possible. The aim is to create such a great first impression that the walk-in customer will return even if you couldn't book them for a treatment that day.

Mistake three: hanging out at the reception desk

Therapists who aren't working at the desk shouldn't hang out in the reception area. It sends a message to customers that the salon isn't very busy and that the therapists have nothing better to do. Also, clients waiting in the reception area can hear everything the staff at the desk say. Recently, a therapist went for an interview at a spa and overheard a conversation between the manager and another staff member. Based on their conversation, the therapist decided this wasn't a place where she wanted to work. Imagine how many customers might be put off by a similar conversation?

Mistake four: eating and drinking at reception

There are still therapists and front of house staff guilty of eating and drinking at reception. Staying hydrated with water is necessary, but other drinks and food aren't acceptable.

Mistake five: not making the clients feel welcome

Have you ever opened the door of your home to someone and then ignored them? No. You wouldn't dream of doing that. Yet, some reception staff don't welcome clients the moment they come through the door. A simple nod of acknowledgement will suffice if you're on the phone. But don't let the client stand aimlessly at reception until you finish your conversation. When a client walks through the door, the first seven seconds are the most important. Make sure you're the reason for a great first impression and for making them feel welcome.

Mistake six: not treating every client like a VIP

Whether the client is a high-profile celebrity or a student, make sure they get the five-star treatment. When I was about ten or eleven years old, my friend and I used to visit a bridal shop in Cape Town and look at all the beautiful tiaras and wedding dresses. To this day, I remember how kind the lady working in the shop was. She always let us try on the tiaras. It would have been easy for her to show us the door. Instead, she treated us so exceptionally that it made an impression on me I've never forgotten.

Mistake seven: not inviting the customer to return

Often, therapists and reception staff simply let clients pay and walk out the door. The best way to secure repeat customers is to book them for a future treatment. Use the client's name and be sure to thank them for their business. It sounds obvious, but not a lot of therapists thank clients for their custom.

Retail counter therapist

The checklist below will help you assess your suitability for working at a luxury beauty counter in a department store.

What qualities do you need to be a successful retail counter therapist?

- **Go-getter.** You need to be someone who likes to make things happen. If you have previous experience exceeding sales targets this would be an advantage.

- **Personal presentation.** Working as a brand ambassador means you are representing the brand and need to be well groomed.

- **Sociable.** You must love playing a key part in special in-store events where you are promoting treatments and products and communicating with a variety of customers.

- **Operational skills.** You're okay with cleaning shelves, unpacking orders, and restocking products, ensuring the counter is kept tidy at all times.

- **IT capability.** You don't mind working on the till, taking payments, and completing opening and closing procedures.

- **Confident.** You will be confident and don't mind traffic-stopping to introduce customers to a new product.

- **Customer service.** You must be someone who prides themselves on their customer service and have a flair for dealing with people.

- **Upbeat.** You will have a positive and cheery personality and love working in a fast-paced environment.

- **Flexibility.** You have a flexible approach and don't mind working evenings and weekends.

Counter manager

As counter manager you will have in-depth skincare knowledge and a real passion that will help drive sales. You should have previous experience working on a skincare counter to enable you to lead by example and deal with daily challenges. You will need to be commercially minded, ensuring the counter is profitable and sales opportunities are maximised.

Let's look at the responsibilities that will be part of your job description:

- **Mentoring.** You will need to mentor and motivate staff to achieve targets, ensuring your team reach their financial goals.

- **Recruitment and development.** Ensure correct staffing levels to deliver the best possible service to clients. Training and development of the team on company policies and procedures.

- **Driving sales.** As counter manager you will be the driving force behind sales results. You will need to analyse business performance to monitor staff productivity.

- **Customer service.** You need to be professional at all times and ensure the team deliver consistently high levels of customer service and assist customers in a friendly and timely manner.

- **Sales campaigns.** Your role will involve executing seasonal promotions and offers and ensuring the team are up to date with new products and offerings.

- **Counter operations.** You will ensure accurate stock take, presentation and replenishment of stock.

- **Profit and loss accountability.** You will have financial responsibilities and report to head office regarding the achievement of retail objectives.

Sales rep/brand ambassador

Being a sales representative or brand ambassador for a skincare company or beauty brand means that you need to be great at two things: networking and sales.

Other responsibilities that will be part of your role include:

- **Targets.** You will be set personal targets that you will need to achieve.

- **Connecting.** You will need to connect with customers in a way that drives sales.

- **Public speaking.** You will need the confidence to demonstrate products and treatment procedures to groups of people.

- **Customer service.** High levels of consistent customer service will be required.

- **Follow-ups.** Your efficiency in the follow-up on sales calls and enquiries will have an impact on your sales.

- **Travel.** You need to be able to travel to clients. If you like to be based in one place, then working as a sales rep or brand ambassador might not suit you.

- **Flexibility.** The role requires a large degree of flexibility and being available some evenings and weekends to accommodate trade shows, client events and product launches.

The six must-have qualities to be a successful sales rep/brand ambassador are:

- **Great communicator.** Communication and confidence are key when you are representing a brand. People that flourish as sales reps and brand ambassadors are those that ask questions and find it easy to connect with others.

- **Good listener.** Sales is about listening: listening to the problems your clients are experiencing in order to provide solutions for them.

- **Positive attitude.** A happy and positive mind-set is needed when working in a sales environment.

- **Meticulous.** Sales is about numbers, so you need to be accurate in financial reporting to head office.

- **Target driven.** You need to be self-motivated and goal-orientated to achieve sales targets and goals.

- **Well presented.** People tend to judge a book by its cover in the beauty industry so being well presented and taking care of yourself is important when you are representing a brand.

Office/sales coordinator

Often, a beauty or skincare company's head office requires help with administration and sales. Clinics with multiple locations might centralise their bookings so all the calls are handled by a few dedicated employees who deal with the enquiries and convert these into sales. These companies prefer ex-therapists who can really promote and sell their products and treatments as they are responsible for taking calls and processing orders. Ultimately, this type of role is about sales and converting leads.

To be successful in a role like this, you need in-depth knowledge of the products and treatments. You also need to know who would benefit from particular treatments, who should avoid particular treatments, and what results the clients can expect. Typically, your role will involve communications, sales, business administration, financial reporting, and distribution (if the company sells products).

What does it take to be a successful office/sales coordinator?

- **Communication skills.** You will need excellent oral, verbal and written skills as you are often the first point of contact for new customers.

- **Telephone manner.** A friendly and welcoming tone is essential to create a great first impression and put customers at ease.

- **Organisational skills.** You need to be organised to ensure the day runs smoothly and efficiently. Excellent time management is needed and high levels of structure.

- **Attention to detail.** It will be part of your role to ensure the small details are taken care of. Ensure that tasks are completed with thoroughness and accuracy.

- **In-depth knowledge.** You will need accurate knowledge of products, treatments and contraindications to assist and advise clients on the most suitable treatments for them.

- **A can-do attitude.** You must be able to deal with challenges and have a knack for problem-solving.

- **Results-driven.** Your role will involve converting enquiries into sales and meticulous financial reporting.

- **Confidence.** Having the confidence to sell and up-sell treatments, packages and products is crucial to becoming a successful office/sales coordinator.

Business development manager

When companies ask us to recruit a business development manager, they ask for someone with strong business acumen who is motivated and driven. Business development managers are responsible for business growth and need to drive sales and exceed targets.

In any given day, you will need to:

- Identify new business opportunities

- Manage and develop the client base

- Connect with new sales leads

- Set up meetings

- Prepare for meetings and engage in strategic planning

- Present products to prospective clients

- Drive revenue and profit

- Report to management

Companies look for the following qualities when they interview potential candidates for the role as business development manager:

- **Previous experience.** Ideally you would have worked for a competitor or within a sales environment and have a proven sales track record. Companies prefer someone who has a big network of contacts.

- **Interpersonal skills.** As business development manager you will be dealing with the decision makers in the company. Social skills and a professional approach is vital to excel in the role.

- **Negotiation skills.** Part of the sales process is negotiation and communication. Business development managers need these skills to thrive.

- **On brand.** Companies want to recruit like-minded people who share their philosophy and can be a true brand ambassador for the business.

- **Results-driven approach.** You need to have a winning mind-set and love the buzz you get from making a sale or closing a deal.

- **Industry knowledge.** Expert knowledge of the industry, treatments, products, and trends are required to be on top of your game as a business development manager.

Lecturer/trainer

Teaching others requires more than just in-depth knowledge on a subject. It requires someone who is truly committed to the job and passionate about helping others. Think back to when you were at school or college. How many teachers stand out? Probably only one or two, right? These teachers had something magical. Somehow, they made the subject more fun, and they brought out the best in you. They made you want to do well. These teachers inspired you, and they cared enough to push you out of your comfort zone.

I asked Rhian Thomas, a CIBTAC accredited tutor and founder of Oh So Lovely, what advice she would give therapists wanting to become lecturers. Rhian suggested approaching a local college to see if they need volunteer assistants in their beauty department. Volunteering this way will give you insight into the day-to-day activities and help you decide if lecturing is a good match for you before you embark on a teacher training course. I also asked Rhian what nobody tells people about lecturing when they start out. She said ultimately, you just have to be yourself and let your love and passion shine through.

Rhian has been a tutor since 2008, and I asked her to what she attributes her success. She said continued research – she keeps up to date with industry trends. As well, she's always well-prepared for her classes. She said the fact that she's still hands-on with clients has helped, too. Then I asked her what traits someone needs to be a great lecturer who makes a significant impact on learners. She said *you need patience, a calm energy, passion, enthusiasm, and great communication skills*, so students gain a clear understanding. Rhian also said *good time management skills are essential.*

Finally, I asked Rhian about the most rewarding aspect of her job as a tutor, and she said that what gives her the most satisfaction is seeing her students develop and grow in confidence after a day in class.

CHAPTER NINE

Starting Your Own Business

Six things you should know before you start your own business

The past summer my recruitment agency was asked by one of the beauty colleges in London to attend their career day and advise students on options available to them. I asked the students a series of questions and 92 per cent said that they wanted to have their own businesses in the future. Being your own boss can take on various forms and in this chapter we discuss popular routes you can take in the industry.

You need to believe in yourself

If you're planning to work for yourself, you need to believe in yourself – believe that you can do it. This quote from Steve Jobs sums up self-belief and how sometimes you just have to trust that things will work out:

> 'You have to trust that the dots will somehow connect in your future. Because believing that the dots will connect down the road will give you the confidence to follow your heart, even when it leads you off the well-worn path.'

You need guts

When I was young, I had a sticker on my pencil case that said 'No guts, no glory'. It was meant for a surfboard, but it reminded me every day that if you don't try, you don't succeed. In business, we need guts – especially when starting out. We need the courage to get going and also the courage to keep going when things get tough. The first part of starting a business is the honeymoon period, when we're excitedly planning. Once we hit the sales phase and things seem to slow down and lose momentum, we need grit and stickability.

It can be relentless

Setting up a business can be relentless, and at times you may long for the eight-hour shifts you used to work when you were employed. Being an entrepreneur means you'll work harder than you've ever worked before. That's why it's so important to be truly passionate about what you're doing.

You need to be resourceful

Entrepreneurs need to be resourceful. The ability to think outside the box to find solutions to problems is a great asset. When you set up a business, your budget might be limited, so the more creative thinking you can apply, the further you'll stretch the budget to create the same result.

You need to be flexible

Being flexible and changing products or services when they no longer serve your clients can make the difference between thriving and just surviving. Trends and downturns in the market will sometimes require you to be proactive and change direction. Don't get too hung up on plan A.

Support and mentorship is powerful

Have a mentor who can support you on your journey – someone who can help you navigate the challenges as you grow and develop your business.

Working from home

A friend of mine is an accomplished therapist who works in a five-star hotel. She's been thinking about doing treatments from home, and we've discussed how she could build a client base. Approaching the hotel's clients would be unethical, and do check your employment contract to ensure there are no restrictions on providing treatments at your home. A good first step for her would be to continue her work at the hotel but cut down on her hours in order to dedicate certain days to her own clients.

If you choose to follow the same path, it's important to make sure your reduced salary will pay the rent and other bills while you build up your home business. If you have a limited marketing budget, start with the people you know. Make a list of everyone you know in your area and from that list pick five people who might be interested in your treatments. Offer them a free treatment and ask that in return, they write a testimonial for you and give five of their friends your price list with an introductory offer to be used within thirty days. After you've completed the treatments with these friends, extend the offer to five of their friends as well, and ask them for testimonials you can use on your website and on social media. Once you're established, consider offering seasonal promotions.

From the moment clients make contact with you, provide remarkable service. It's likely that they're already having treatments elsewhere. You have to think about what sets you apart from other therapists. What can you offer and what is your unique selling point? Think of how you can stand out from the competition. Limit the treatments that you offer. Become an expert and have people come to you not because you're an all-round therapist but because you're the best at providing a particular treatment. Think about the treatments you love doing. If facials are your thing, consider what skincare brand would be a good partner for you. Are you going to use machines or keep it hands-on? Initially, you want to keep your spending as low as possible. As you make money, you can reinvest in the business. Keep things simple and see what works. Make adjustments and tweak as you go along.

If you have only a studio apartment, you can still make it work by using screens to separate your treatment area. Make use of aroma mist diffusers to create a feeling of calm and tranquillity. Lighting is an important factor, especially if you're offering relaxing treatments such as massage. Ideally, you want to layer the lighting. This means having different lights at different levels. You might dim your ceiling lights and have a floor light or table light to create ambiance. Lighting can dramatically change the mood of the room, especially if it's layered. If you offer treatments such as lash extensions, microblading, or make-up, you need to ensure that your room is bright enough, so you can focus on details. If you're lucky enough to have a spare room to use for your treatments, choose a colour scheme that creates a feeling of serenity.

With new clients, it's important to begin with a thorough consultation to understand their needs and truly cater to them. If they get results, they'll come back. I have a friend who is a skin expert. She works for herself and is constantly thinking of ways she can get the best results for her customers. She creates bespoke treatments and charges a premium for these. She's also active on Instagram and posts before and after pictures of clients, photos of the products that she uses, and expert skin tips and advice. As well, she frequently goes on training courses. When you work for yourself, it's important to keep investing in yourself. Go on courses and keep learning so you can share information with your clients and provide them with a better service.

Renting a room

If you prefer to be based in one place and don't like the idea of having clients come to your home, renting a room is a good option. Normally, you'll pay either a monthly flat rate or a percentage of your income. Popular percentages are 70/30, 60/40, and 50/50. If everything is included and you just have to turn up and do the treatments, it's likely the salon or clinic owner will take 70 per cent of your income. They'll provide you with all the products and a fully equipped room, and will do your marketing. They'll also take all the bookings and payments on your behalf, and at the end of the month you'll invoice the salon 30 per cent of the income you generated. If you take 50 or

60 per cent of the income, you'll have to provide your own products and equipment. You and the salon or clinic owner will negotiate how your clients will make bookings and who will take payment at the end of their treatments.

Renting a room can be a good way to start out, especially if the salon is well established and you can introduce your services to their clients. To promote yourself, consider presenting your services when the salon has an open evening. Prepare a short pitch and offer a discount if clients make a booking on that night. This way, you start with clients already booked in. Once those clients come to see you, be sure to give them referral vouchers. Ensure that your marketing material is ready on the night. A good idea is to have a goody bag you can give to those who attend. Some people might need a bit longer to make a buying decision, so a goody bag with your brochure will be a great reminder for them. Be creative and think of what else you could include in the goody bag.

When you present your pitch, bear the following in mind to make an impact:

- **Who**

  Say your name and what treatments you specialise in. Clients want to have treatments with the best person for the job. If you specialise in brow treatments, introduce yourself as a brow expert.

- **Why**

  Think about why clients should come to you for treatments. Say how long you've been working in the industry. If you've worked at well-known salons, clinics, or hotels, mention this. If you've been mentioned in the press or voted as a top therapist, this is the time to say so.

- **What**

  Think of the clients who come to see you and what problems they have. Is there something that a lot of them struggle with or wish they could improve? You want to become an expert in your clients' problems. If you are a skin expert, you might say in your pitch that typically your clients want flawless and glowing skin and not to look tired.

- **Outcomes**

  What outcomes would your clients like to achieve? Talk about how you will address their concerns and provide solutions for them. This is where you would tell the clients the treatments you could offer that would give them that dewy skin that looks like they are just back from a week's relaxing holiday.

- **Big picture**

  What does the big picture look like? What is your vision in the world? Think how you could make a greater impact on others, and not just by helping your own clients. Perhaps your vision is to donate money to a charity that specialises in burn victims so as a skin expert you can make a difference on a global scale?

The idea of your pitch is to get you to the next step. The next step might not be an immediate sale. The next step might be a conversation where a potential client asks for your advice about skin concerns. This is an opportunity to book them in for a consultation and suggest a treatment plan to address their concerns.

The downside of renting a room is that your working hours will be dictated by the salon's hours. Initially, you might have to spend a lot of money on equipment, if you're responsible for providing this. The upside is that you'll be collaborating with the salon, and in doing so, you'll receive inside information about their clients and their behaviour, which will help you build a marketing strategy to match your audience.

If you don't fancy the idea of renting a room within a hair salon or holistic practice, renting a room within a large corporate company might appeal to you. Often, companies have an on-site gym but don't offer treatments. This is ideal, as it provides you with a base of potential clients. Massage is a popular treatment in this type of environment, so advertising this service would be beneficial to you. This time, you would be pitching to the company – sell them on why they should let space to you. Your *who*, *why*, and *big picture* will stay the same, but the *what* and *outcome* will be different.

Mobile beauty therapist

Mobile therapists work when it suits them. This is ideal if you're juggling childcare or other responsibilities. You can target different groups of people depending on the day and time. During the week, you could promote yourself to corporates and offer thirty-minute mini-treatments that people could fit into their lunch hour. You will need to arrange a private space in a conference room or office to set up your treatment bed or manicure table. The benefit of working with corporates is that you can get your day fully booked ahead of time. Ask if you can have a regular slot, say once a month, at their offices. That way you have guaranteed work.

Companies are very aware of staff health and the impact it has on the workplace. You could work with the HR department and put together a well-being package. The company could pay for their staff to have treatments or they could subsidise them, as they do with the staff canteen.

Another idea is to partner with care homes to provide treatments to people who might not be able to go to a salon or spa due to immobility. Again, set up a regular slot so you can make bookings in advance.

You'll be able to make a real difference in people's lives. The biggest disease of our time is loneliness, so you'll be doing much more than just providing a treatment.

You could even offer a package to new moms who can't go to the salon. Providing them with treatments in the comfort of their own homes will remove the childcare worry. Finally, if you're available on weekends, the party scene is big – spa parties for kids or pamper parties for baby showers and hen dos.

The downside of being a mobile therapist is that you have to cart your equipment around. It's much easier logistically if you have a car. You also have to factor in time between appointments to get from A to B, as well as time to set up and pack up. The longer you're in one place, the more financially viable it is. If you're going to private homes, think of what add-ons you could offer. For example, if your client has booked a facial, suggest a brow tint and shape or a set of lashes to really make an impact and to make the appointment more financially viable for you.

Being a mobile therapist means you need to promote and market yourself well, as you won't have a salon or clinic to do this for you. You'll also need to be very organised. Prepare a bag that contains everything you might need for the day, every day. And be prepared to work evenings.

A good mobile therapist is confident, polite, and respectful and should be prepared to sign an NDA (non-disclosure agreement, also known as a confidentiality agreement).

If you love travelling and are flexible in terms of time, you could promote yourself as a therapist to high-net-worth individuals who travel a lot and want a therapist on hand to provide treatments while they're on location. You'll need to build your profile if you want to go down this route. When these clients search the internet, be the one who appears as the 'go-to' private therapist. Focus on building your brand, which is you. You might find yourself working around the globe or on super yachts.

Freelance beauty temp

A beauty temp works with agencies who find work for them. They usually have their own private clients as well, so this works well for mobile therapists. The advantage of being a beauty temp is that you don't have to find your own clients. You don't have to do any marketing or advertising, so you'll save yourself a lot of money and time.

As a temp, you'll work in a variety of places, from salons and spas to hotels and clinics. It will provide you with insight into how various establishments run. You'll get the opportunity to work with different kinds of people, and no two days will ever be the same.

You must be prepared to travel to various locations and be okay with being the new kid on the block. Every day will be like the first day at a new job, but you quickly adapt. I wouldn't advise temping unless you have at least five years' experience under your belt since qualifying.

Another advantage of being a beauty temp is that you're in charge of your schedule. You choose which days you want to work. Also, you choose when you go on holiday, and you won't have to try to fit in clients before you go. You simply don't make yourself available for bookings.

Successful temps are reliable and turn up early for their shifts. The clients want you to fit in seamlessly with their company. They don't want their clients to know that you're a temp. For that day, you're part of their team. That's why it's important to turn up early so you can ask how things work and how they like things done.

Universal rules apply to all salons and spas, regardless of their size or location.

- **Turn off your phone and leave it in your bag.** Seeing therapists on their phones is a pet hate of managers and owners.

- **Look the part.** Present yourself immaculately (if you have long hair, tie it up). People judge books by their cover, especially in the beauty industry, so make sure you present yourself in the best possible way.

- **Avoid confusion.** Introduce yourself to the clients and confirm what treatment you're providing them.

- **Check for contraindications before commencing any treatment.** At the start of the day, ask the salon or spa to provide you with consultation forms for the client to sign.

- **Get the clients to sign the forms.** Some might be reluctant, but this is imperative for health, safety, and insurance reasons.

- **Determine the needs of the client and provide the best treatments possible.** Client satisfaction is your primary aim when you're a temp.

- **Be professional at all times.** Be calm and polite.

- **Go the extra mile.** If you don't have a treatment booked in, ask the manager or owner if they need help with anything. This will set you apart from other temps.

- **Tidy the room after your treatment.** Leave it spotless. When you arrive, you may find that the room is unmade. Complaining about this is not going to get you brownie points. Instead, tidy the room and get on with your day.

- **Thank the salon or spa manager at the end of your day,** just as you would if you'd been invited to someone's home for the day. This is a polite way to build a good relationship with them.

Setting up a beauty salon

New salons open every week. How can you ensure yours is a success? Apply these six rules to help you set up a profitable salon.

Rule one: determine your ideal clients

This is one of the most important aspects of setting up your salon. Without clients, you have no business. Once you know who your ideal clients are, the whole process will be much easier. Ask yourself, 'Who would be a delight to work with?' You must be able to visualise your ideal clients.

- Who are they?

- How old are they?

- Where do they live?

- Where do they shop?

- Do they work, study, or raise children? Are they retired?

You need to be specific – remember, you're building a business around your ideal clients.

One of the salons we work with has identified exactly who their ideal customer is. She's female, has money to spend on herself, lives in a beautiful home, travels a lot, and loves having treatments. The salon owner has built her whole business around this person. When you walk into the salon, you're immediately greeted by beautiful aromas. Their ideal client burns candles in her home every day and always has fresh flowers. The environment includes velvet sofas, the latest fashion and interior design magazines, and gorgeous soft furnishings. The salon brews tea with fresh ginger, lemon, and spices. The whole experience is one of utter luxury and pampering. Each step of the client journey has been created with the salon's ideal client in mind and what this person likes. The salon is thriving, and has won several awards.

Then there are those who don't manage to get the ideal client matrix right. I once met a woman who rented the whole downstairs of a hairdressing salon for her skin clinic. The idea was to tap into the hairdressers' client base. The salon had a great footfall and had been established for over fifteen years. On paper, it seemed like a good match. But the clinic's ideal clients were people who spent a lot of money on their skin. The hairdressing business offered cheap haircuts and attracted clients who wanted a cheap and cheerful service. Needless to say, the clinic's clients and the salon's clients were opposite types. It simply didn't work, and the clinic didn't survive. If you're partnering with another business, make sure your ideal clients and their clients are the same people. It can make or break your business.

Rule two: choose a great location

Location is key when setting up your salon. Don't compromise on this. Choose a location in the area where your ideal clients live or work, and ensure the area has a great footfall and the premises are visible. Enlist the help of a commercial agent who knows of properties before they're on the market. Here are a few things to do when choosing a location:

- Find out the length of the lease of the property

- Ask if there's a rent-free period

- Negotiate a break clause, so you have a financial safety net

- Find out from the landlord about rent-review or rent-increase policies

- Find out how much the deposit is

- Determine the internal and external responsibilities you'll have as the tenant

- Clarify how you must leave the premises at the end of the tenancy

- Find out what business rates you'll need to pay

Rule three: create a brand

A brand isn't a logo. A brand is your company's identity. It's your values and what you stand for. In essence, your brand is your reputation. In business today, your reputation is everything. Your success is built on reputation.

A component of your brand is your company name. Some companies use family names. Estée Lauder did just that. Others choose names with meaning. Some companies, like Facebook, combine two words. Others go for descriptions (i.e. the name conveys a feeling or describes something). And some companies, such as Häagen Daz, use made-up words. Once you've decided on your company name, you must check to see if the domain name is available to buy. Shireen Smith, an intellectual property law expert, says that if you want the name to function as a trademark, it needs to be distinctive rather than descriptive, available to use, and legally effective.

Colours are another part of your brand. There is an entire school of psychology around colour, so choose one that will reflect what you stand for.

Yellow: optimism, warmth

Orange: vitality, joy, happiness

Red: energy, boldness

Green: health, nature, growth, freshness

Blue: dependability, security

Purple: creativity, prestige

Multicolour: multidisciplinary, informality, fun

The key with branding is consistency across all platforms. It's worth paying a brand expert to help you with your brand strategy and your brand story. In the past, some companies were faceless, but now, people want to know there's a person behind the brand. Make sure you're visible.

Rule four: choose your top products and treatments

You need to decide which products you'll use in the salon and what treatments you'll offer. Ask yourself what problems and concerns your ideal clients have and what solutions you can offer them. Establish what product range will help you solve your clients' problems and give the best results.

Don't try to be all things to all people. Decide whether you want to focus on skincare, holistic beauty, aesthetic treatments, nails, brows and lashes, or waxing. You must create a unique selling point so that your salon stands out. Think of what would make your salon different and create a signature treatment. You should offer high-value treatments that are profitable. Make sure you experience the treatments yourself before you shortlist skincare companies to partner with.

TIP

You need to determine the best match for your business, so ask potential product house representatives the following questions.

- What is the opening order amount and minimum ongoing spend?
- Will there be regular salon visits and assistance with open evenings?
- What training is included?
- Will gifts to use as incentives be provided?
- What merchandise will be provided?

Rule five: market yourself

Get your website and social media profiles up and running before your salon opens. You want to create a lot of content that you can publish. On your website, don't just list the treatments – explain the benefits of each treatment. Have a video demonstrating the treatments so that potential customers can see what they entail. This is particularly useful for potential clients who have never had them. Before and after pictures are a great way to sell a treatment. This way, customers can see the results. Have testimonials from clients to give potential customers peace of mind when they book a treatment. It's also useful to have additional information about the treatment, such as:

- Length of time the treatment takes

- Pain factor (especially useful to know for advanced skin treatments)

- Downtime required (so clients can plan the rest of their day)

- Aftercare advice

Make a launch party part of your marketing strategy. Invite bloggers and journalists to get word out that there's a new salon in town. Demonstrations or taster sessions will give potential customers an opportunity to experience the treatments. Ensure you provide people with an incentive to book a treatment at the launch party for a future date. Your goody bag should include your price list, a voucher for the first treatment, and information about the products. Any products you can include will be a great boost. The strategy of the launch party is to introduce your ideal clients to your business and to get them booked in so that when the salon opens its doors, you start with bookings already in the diary.

Rule six: design for first impressions

The moment clients come through the door, wow them. You can make a big impact with colour and lighting. Colour is the most powerful way to transform a room, and lighting is the most powerful way to create atmosphere. A feature wall will add interest and give the room depth, especially if the room has a boxy feel. It's easy to create a focal point using paint, wallpaper, or wooden floorboards on the wall. If you're trying to create atmosphere, position lights on the floor but behind a sofa or chairs, where they aren't visible. They'll project the light upwards to create a beautiful glow.

If you're charging premium prices, the salon has to look a certain way. Remember, always design with your ideal clients in mind. Create a space they want to return to. Time and time again. A space where they feel they can have an hour or two of 'me time' – where they can relax, unwind, and get results.

CHAPTER TEN

Success Strategies

Twelve hacks for success

Why are some people more successful than others? Are they more intelligent? Do they have better ideas? Have they just been lucky? Successful people share certain traits and practise certain habits on a daily basis. The following actions will help guide you to success.

1. **Find your passion**

   You have to love what you do. If you don't love your work enough, you'll want to give up. When you love what you do, it often won't feel like work. It will feel as though you're making a difference in the world and helping others, and this will provide a huge amount of satisfaction. Your passion is what gives you purpose.

2. Persevere

When the going gets tough, keep going. Achieving success isn't easy; even if you love what you do, it's going to be tough sometimes. If you feel like giving up, think about why you started. Just keep on plugging away and you'll reap the benefits. When you want to give up, this is precisely the time when you need to keep going. Success and persistence go hand in hand.

3. Work hard

There is no substitute for hard work. Can you name one person who became an overnight success? Everyone who is successful has put in hours and hours of hard work. To be successful, you need to execute plans to make things happen. Many people have fantastic ideas but only a handful of people bring them to fruition. Success is linked to action. If you have an idea, something you're passionate about, act on it. Make a start. If you don't, you'll never know what you could have accomplished.

4. Have patience

It may seem strange to see patience on a checklist for success. We live in a time where everything is instant – you can have everything you want within a few clicks of your phone. But success doesn't operate that way. You have to learn to be patient if you want to achieve your goals.

5. Read! Read! Read!

Read as much as you can. Warren Buffett is one of the richest men in the world, and he credits his success to nurturing his habit of daily reading. He believes that daily reading enables you to build up a wealth of ideas and strategies. In fact, most successful people say that reading is an invaluable ingredient of their success.

6. Prioritise your health

Your health determines the quality of your life. If you lead a healthy life, you'll have more energy and will achieve more. When you're fit and healthy, you can deal with challenges far better and handle the curveballs life throws at you.

7. Don't make excuses

If you want to make something happen, just do it. Forget about the excuses of not having enough time, money, or connections. If you want to make it happen, you'll find a way. Otherwise, you'll find excuses. Success is connected to action, so instead of making excuses, make a start.

8. Surround yourself with inspiring people

Jim Rohn said,

'You are the average of the five people you spend the most time with.'

I love this quote. Think of the people around you. Do you surround yourself with people who don't like their work, who have no ambition to improve themselves? Think of which friends lift you up and which ones drag you down. Spend less time with those who drain you of your energy and more time with those who inspire you and enhance your life. If you want to be remarkable, you must surround yourself with remarkable people.

9. Have a purpose

Don't just do things for the sake of it. Have a purpose. If you know why you're doing what you're doing, your work will become more meaningful and fulfilling. Think bigger than yourself. Consider how you can make a difference to others and to the world we live in.

10. Be courageous

If you want to be successful, you must be prepared to take calculated risks. You must believe in yourself and your abilities. Celebrate the small wins; each achievement will give you the confidence to go on and achieve more.

11. Never stop learning

Nelson Mandela said,

> 'Education is the most powerful weapon which you can use to change the world.'

If you want to be successful, you must keep on learning and expanding your knowledge. Learn from others. Constant improvement is key. Always be on the lookout for hot topics and trends so that you can evolve.

12. Have fun

Business has to be fun as well – if it's not, you're in the wrong game. As Andrew Carnegie said,

> 'There is little success where there is little laughter.'

Tips from the top

Over the years I've met some truly remarkable people in business. I'd like to share with you tips from a few industry experts who have not only been successful in business but have also inspired others on their journey to success.

I first met **Robin Mauras Cartier** just before he became regional spa director for AccorHotels in Asia. As regional spa director for The Set Hotels, Robin played an instrumental part in the Akasha Holistic Wellbeing Centre, at Hotel Café Royal, winning several awards and accolades. Under his direction, it was voted as England's Best Hotel Spa at the World Spa Awards 2017. It's fair to say Robin knows a thing or two about running successful spas.

I asked Robin to what he attributed his success, and he said curiosity, a desire to learn, hard work, and knowing how to utilise the skills of the people around him. He's passionate about the industry and it shows. He manages his team with integrity and a strong work ethic, and they respect him for it. He has a fair and open style of communication. His transparent approach works well, as he creates a team with spirit and that consistently provides high-quality service.

I also asked Robin what advice he would give to therapists wanting to be successful, and he recommended that they keep on learning by learning from others, learning new techniques, and learning about psychology. He went on to say that getting international experience is great for personal development, as life experience is extremely valuable in the industry.

'Always aim for the best and be consistent in delivering an amazing experience. Empathy is very important, and good therapists should truly love people and their jobs. A good therapist must want to make a difference in people's lives.'

Robin emphasised that not all therapists are suited to the same environment. Some might prefer hotel spas, others day spas or medi-spas, so it's important to find out what suits you the best so you can evolve, make a difference, and follow your chosen path.

Louise Stewart founded Nakedhealth MEDISPA in 2004, and I met her shortly after. Nakedhealth was one of the first medi-spas in the UK, and today it's still a front-runner in the industry, providing a comprehensive range of treatments in state-of-the-art facilities. Its client base continues to grow.

I asked Louise about the importance of consistency in the workplace and the role it plays in achieving long-term success. Louise shared that consistency in care is essential so that the client experience is similar at every visit. This relates to treatment protocols as well as to the level of service clients receive. Louise explained that clients want to see the same person each time they come in, and that building a strong rapport is vital. Therefore, keeping a motivated and happy team is extremely important.

At Nakedhealth, the staff are loyal, and staff retention is high. I asked Louise what she looks for when she takes on a new team member. She replied, 'There is no single attribute. An appetite for learning new skills, an enthusiasm for the industry, a manner which is engaging and interested. Someone who listens and asks questions.'

When I asked Louise if she would share some tips to help therapists and budding clinic managers, she advised first and foremost to treat everyone equally, with respect and dignity. She emphasised the importance of only selling treatments and products which are appropriate to your clients' needs, as you won't build loyal customers unless you offer them good outcomes. Louise recommended that managers share the company goals with their team and work with them to achieve these goals. Finally, she said one should never judge people by their clothes, cars, or chat. You'd be surprised by who turns out to be the best clients.

Sunita Passi is the founder of the award-winning Ayurveda companies Tri-Dosha and NEEM Sunita Passi. I met Sunita years ago at a networking event, and we swapped business cards.

I asked Sunita what inspired her to start her own product range, and she explained that she'd initially imported traditional Ayurvedic oils from India to facilitate her Ayurvedic therapy training programmes. She said that they'd seen some level of success, but more and more clients started to ask if there was an Ayurvedic range that didn't smell so pungent. This gave her the confidence to develop her own range. Sunita said she thought if customers had asked for this, then it was a good sign.

Sunita started with body and massage oils, and for two years focused primarily on these products. Then, a client in Ireland commented on how much she loved the company's marma (vital point) face massage and felt that it would be an even better treatment if there was a skincare range to go with it. Inspired by these words, Sunita set out to develop one. The bath products came to life when they launched their treatment range within a boutique spa hotel in the UK. Today, Sunita's company is one of the leading Ayurveda brands and is sold in many countries around the world.

Sunita's certified training programmes have inspired numerous therapists to start their own businesses. I wanted to know Sunita's top tips for a therapist wanting to be the best. She advised to schedule time for new training and to choose therapies that align with your own philosophical and spiritual orientation. She highlighted the importance of unplugging for a time, as we give so much as therapists. We need to make sure we take time to relax and rejuvenate. Making time for a holiday every year and having something to look forward to is imperative. Sunita recommended eliminating the excess, and to reflect on and be honest about what's working in your business and what isn't. Highlight the stuff you need to cut out. This leaves more room to be creative and innovative.

I asked Sunita what advice she would give to her eighteen-year-old self, and she said, 'Be guided by your passion.' She advocates the importance of finding good business mentors to advise you – people who really understand what it is you're looking to create, and why you're creating it. Having mentors gives you the confidence to try new things, brainstorm new ideas, and move to success more quickly and efficiently.

Helen Merchant is an international spa consultant who studied business and finance before completing her CIBTAC and CIDESCO diplomas. I asked Helen how important it is for therapists to understand finance and the basics of profit and loss. She explained that it's essential to understand cost versus revenue, and to understand efficient occupancy and maximum returns. She advises therapists not to be afraid of figures but to break them down into manageable amounts: the number of treatments you need to perform or the number of products you need to sell to achieve your targets.

After finishing her beauty studies, Helen held the positions of therapist and senior therapist for four years before taking on a management role. While Helen was working as a therapist, her column was fully booked three months in advance. She explained that returning clients come back because of the quality and the expertise of the therapist who is treating them. Her advice is to become an expert therapist and only then take the step into management. This way, you can lead by example and inspire your team to become experts, which leads to a successful spa operation.

At one stage of her career, Helen was fleet training and development manager on board a cruise liner, and one of her responsibilities was training and developing spa managers. I asked her about this experience and what tips she would give to someone thinking of working on board a cruise liner. Helen said this is a tough role, and one of the hardest to adjust to. It challenges managers to think outside the box to achieve budgets. She found that motivating the team was key in this environment. She said she would encourage anyone looking for a new experience to work on ships, as it's fun and lifelong friendships are made. She went on to explain that although the living conditions are tough and it's physically hard work, the pay can be excellent.

Helen also said that confidence plays a big part in selling. Your confidence in your abilities will instil trust in your clients. They will believe in your recommendations and see you as an expert.

Helen worked for Six Senses Spas across Asia, the Middle East, and Europe as projects director. She said that therapists looking for medium- to long-term career progression should consider hotel groups – they're a good way to advance your career, as they offer excellent training.

Claire Vero is the founder of Aurelia Probiotic Skincare, and I asked her what inspired her to launch her award-winning skincare range. Claire explained that when her skin became dry and started to change during her twenties and early thirties, she decided that she needed to make a serious change to her skincare routine. She wanted to create a brand that was serious about age prevention and had the data to back it up: a range that catered to all ages and skin types and that would be a complete delight and treat to use on a daily basis.

At the time, there wasn't one single brand that stood out and satisfied all these criteria. She therefore made it her mission to create the ideal range. Her previous work in the pharmaceutical sector and with the Dermatology Centre of Excellence helped her discover probiotics – the unique technology present throughout the range that protects the skin and balances and manages its level of inflammation. From this, she decided to create and launch Aurelia Probiotic Skincare to fit the strict criteria she'd set for a natural, yet scientifically proven, skincare line.

Claire was awarded the CEW (Cosmetic Executive Woman) Achiever Award in 2014, which is an accolade that acknowledges peer admiration in the industry. She was also listed by Management Today as one of the Top 35 People Under 35 to watch. I was curious to know what advice she would give a beauty therapist wanting to win awards and be recognised in the industry.

Claire advised seeking awards that are relevant to you and your field of beauty therapy – don't try to win them all. Hand-pick and prioritise a selection of relevant awards and make sure you're well-prepared when you try for them. Analyse every area of your expertise to ensure that you can really sell your abilities and offerings. She said it's important to make sure that what you offer goes above and beyond expectation.

You need to pay close attention to detail, hone your playlist, decorate your treatment room, and make sure you're always well groomed. Assess your network and client base to ensure you're bettering your chances through all stages.

Aurelia Probiotic Skincare was selected by global online retailer NET-A-PORTER a mere eight weeks after trading started, and as one of just fifteen brands to represent its exclusive launch into beauty. It also retails with Space NK, Liberty and international flagships and boutiques. I asked Claire how the brand had gained such status so quickly. She explained that it was due to their three-point philosophy that focuses on fusing science, nature, and luxury.

I then asked Claire for her top business tips or life lessons. She said that she'd been given the following advice herself: 'No one drives your career forward except you yourself. It's important to make sure that you treat your colleagues and people around you the way you would wish to be treated yourself. Most importantly, respect on all sides is paramount for a business to flourish.'

Sarah Chapman is a skincare authority and London's most sought-after facialist. Sarah created a luxury skincare brand in a competitive market, and I asked her what she attributed her success to. Sarah said determination, professionalism, integrity, hard work, and never taking no for an answer. So many elements come into play when building a successful business:

the quality of your product, the way it looks, how you manage distribution, and marketing and public relations, to name but a few. Sarah said, 'There is always so much to think about and manage, but through all of that the most important thing is to really believe in what you're doing, keep your eye on your goals, and never give up.' It's her belief that anything is possible.

I wanted to know from Sarah how easy it was to set up a business, and whether she'd faced any obstacles along the way. She said she'd been lucky enough to have a number of years' experience as well as diversity within the beauty industry. These gave her a solid understanding of where to start and whom to go to make her vision a reality. She added that her knowledge of developing and running a skincare brand had been limited and that this worked to her advantage – she was able to act and think in an entrepreneurial way rather than follow a format.

That doesn't mean she didn't face challenges, though. Although Sarah had a successful clinic business, the logistics of the product development side were relatively new and the learning curve was therefore steep. Sarah added that it's important not to be too hard on yourself, as you learn from mistakes and this helps you to think outside the box and move forward.

I asked Sarah what advice she would give a therapist wanting to make a name for themselves. Sarah said being a therapist is really hard work and that it's essential to go that extra mile, to really stand out from the crowd; to learn as much as you can, listen to your clients, and never be afraid to develop your own methods based on your personal experiences. If you don't enjoy what you do and genuinely care, your clients will feel that, so make sure you feed your own needs by attending lectures, getting training, reading, and developing yourself.

Sarah has been featured live on QVC and has made regular TV appearances. This led me to asking her what qualities she believes therapists desiring to become brand ambassadors should aim to develop.

'Integrity is incredibly important. I have built my reputation on an honest, no-nonsense approach. It's all about building trust. It's a small industry, and it's important always to be professional and discreet. One negative issue can stay with you for years. Never "put down" another brand or contemporary. Gain credibility on your own merits.'

Sarah went on to say to really represent a brand, it helps to truly love it. People aren't stupid, they can tell if your heart isn't in it, so always find something to love in every brand or product – nothing is quite as contagious as enthusiasm.

Sarah has created multi-award-winning products that are constantly featured in fashion, beauty, and style magazines. I wanted to know why her products are so popular with all the A-listers. Sarah explained that in the beauty industry, reputation is extremely important. So when creating a skincare product, the most important consideration is that the products work. Efficacy is king. Sarah uses her products every day, both at home and in the clinic.

I asked Sarah what career advice she would give beauty therapists wanting to promote themselves and advance their careers. She said to work hard and always do your best, and to go the extra mile when you can, as it does get noticed. As an employer, she values loyalty and commitment and believes it should be rewarded. A commitment to always giving 100%, an ability to listen and take on board information and instructions, and a drive to support your team are attributes that are hard to ignore. Continue self-learning and never expect things to be handed to you on a silver platter, as ultimately, what you put in, you get out.

Finally, I wanted to know what tips Sarah would give to a beauty therapist just starting out. She said be true to yourself. Take opportunities, try lots of different areas, and pursue what you're passionate about. Whether it's holistic therapy, massage, or aesthetics, if you really love what you do, you'll certainly be on the path to success.

Bharat Parmar is the founder of Genco, a London-based chain of male grooming salons. Bharat founded Genco in 2007, when male grooming was still in its infancy. I was curious to know what had prompted him to start a male grooming business. Bharat said he'd noticed that men were beginning to understand the benefits of grooming and were increasingly looking for services other than just a simple haircut. Sporting celebrities, such as David Beckham, were openly talking about their grooming, and this was beginning to make grooming more mainstream. The product companies were starting to launch men's ranges for skincare and haircare, and the market was rapidly growing from a small base. Bharat also recognised that men were looking for a better haircut experience than they were getting at a local barber. He decided to launch a men's salon with the ethos of a top hair and beauty salon but with a service style that was informal (yet professional) and suited men. Bharat said that his guests feel as if they belong to a 'club', and that their visits to Genco aren't a chore but an experience.

From my experience of working with Genco, I know that they take their customer service seriously, so I wanted to know from Bharat if he thought the success of his company was due to the high level of service they provide. Bharat explained that they have an incredibly high return and customer-retention rate plus a high rate of referral – way above the average for a normal salon. This is because they provide a high level of service and the therapists and hairdressers who work for Genco are very skilled. The environment in his salons is impressive but not threatening or overly ostentatious.

I asked Bharat what advice he would give to beauty therapists wishing to make a name for themselves. He said it comes down to customer service and listening to the clients. Bharat recommended projecting yourself into your customer's shoes to understand what they might be thinking. Always be helpful and try to meet their needs. For example, if you can't fit a client in, always offer alternative times and days, and even if you know you won't get a cancellation, always say that you'll call if you do. Bharat said at Genco, they encourage clients to give feedback, and when they fall short (as they know they won't always get it right!), they don't argue with the client. They take the complaint seriously and take appropriate action to make sure the client is happy.

I also wanted to know what business lessons Bharat has learned since setting up Genco. He said always deal in facts and be honest about how you and your company are performing. Listen to advice from others but follow your own instincts as far as you can. Do at least one thing every day to push your company forward. You will always lose clients, so make sure that you have an ongoing marketing programme that drives new customers through the door. If an initiative doesn't work, it doesn't mean that it won't work. You have to understand why it didn't work the first time and then tweak it. Don't leave the marketing to 'when you have time'. It's ultimately the most important thing in any business.

Hannah Scott is national training manager at Decléor and Carita. I asked her what mistakes therapists tend to make in the treatment room, and what could they do to ensure better treatments.

Hannah said common mistakes during treatments can range from not preparing the equipment fully and not setting up correctly to not listening to what the clients want to achieve from their treatments. In her experience, Hannah has found that truly listening to your clients' priorities will ensure that you deliver the best possible treatment to meet their needs and allay their concerns.

Prior to becoming national training manager of Decléor and Carita, Hannah was global e-commerce customer-service supervisor of FitFlop, where she managed customer-service agents across three territories in the UK, EU, and US. I asked her what role customer service plays in the success of a company. She said that customer service is what differentiates you from your competition. In the beauty industry, receiving excellent service is one of the key factors that brings clientele back to your salon. I asked Hannah to share how she ensured customer satisfaction. She said that one should *ask* clients about their concerns and *listen* to their feedback. Many of us ask but don't really listen. This could make the difference between a client returning or not.

During her time as store manager of the largest boutique specialising in waxing and lingerie in

London, Hannah was in charge of the day-to-day operations. I asked her what advice she would give to therapists wanting to make sure their days run smoothly. She recommended establishing efficiency, especially in a business as busy and dynamic as the flagship store she managed. She always had a plan for the day. A great manager sets daily goals and retail targets, so each team member knows what they're responsible for that day, in addition to what they need to achieve as a team. As a therapist, if you don't have a plan for the day with achievable goals, it's extremely difficult to know what's expected of you. She said that therapists should ask their managers for support in keeping them focused and suggested that they be rewarded for achieving personal and team goals.

Hannah started out as a beauty therapist but progressed rapidly through the ranks. This made me curious about what had contributed to her success. She said she's always been dedicated to the industry and that after attending her first Decléor training session, she knew that she wanted to teach, train, and motivate other students. But at eighteen, she had had little experience and knew that to achieve her goal, she had to work in diverse areas to gain the experience in different roles in the industry.

Hannah said that the most important lesson she learned over the years was to never stop learning – she attended as many self-development and industry-related courses as she possibly could, to push herself out of her comfort zone. This is how Hannah progressed in the industry that she loves.

Claire Aggarwal founded Perfect 10 Mobile Beauty, one of London's first mobile beauty businesses, established in 2011. I asked Claire what inspired her to start the business. She said that from a young age she'd wanted to have her own business and believed that the sky was the limit. She believed that hard work paid off and it felt natural to put time and effort into creating her own business. Claire wanted to offer her clients treatments in the comfort of their own homes, as well as to create a corporate division that took care of high-profile events. A few years later, a black-label service was added to the portfolio, specifically designed for high-net-worth individuals and VIPs; it gave them the opportunity to book treatments twenty-four hours a day.

I asked Claire about the most rewarding aspect of her job, and she said it was making the lives of clients easier. I wanted to know why the company had been so successful in a competitive market. Claire attributed their success to company training and customer service. Every therapist received extensive training when they came on board. Claire said that the most important people in the business are the therapists, because happy therapists mean happy clients. Claire established a business where the customer was always right and is sure this is the reason they became the market leader.

I asked Claire about the most important business lesson she has learned over the years. She said that sometimes things go wrong or therapists move on to other careers. This is beyond your control. When it's your own business, it's hard not to take things personally, but she's learned that business is business, and you have to learn to be less sensitive.

I wanted to know what advice Claire would give beauty therapists just starting out, and she advised getting as much experience as possible. There's a common misconception that if you don't have much experience, salons and spas won't hire you. This isn't the case. If you have the right attitude, they will. While you're at college, try to gain experience by offering to work somewhere for free one evening or one day a week. Once you have a well-written CV that lists a few great names, a strong cover letter, and the right attitude, you'll be able to get a job.

Perfect 10 has worked with a lot of celebrity clients, and I wondered whether Claire had any advice for therapists treating VIPs or Hollywood stars. She said, 'Just be yourself.' Celebs are just people, and if you act differently around them, they won't like it. Claire stressed the importance of confidentiality when it comes to dealing with clients. Their A-list celebrities kept on coming back as the company was careful never to reveal anything to the press or media about them.

I asked Claire about the qualities therapists need to become successful mobile beauty therapists. She said first and foremost you need to be hard-working and you need to be prepared to work evenings and weekends. This is the time most clients tend to want a treatment. She recommended that you be organised – you cannot forget to take anything with you. Moreover, you need to be bubbly and polite and you need to be able to read clients well. Making a client feel uncomfortable in a treatment room is far from ideal. Doing this in their home means they'll never ask you back.

Sue West is the general manager and director of HR at The Organic Pharmacy. The first store opened in London in 2002, and today the company has stores and distribution centres all over the world. Sue has interviewed hundreds of therapists throughout her career at The Organic Pharmacy, and I wanted to know what three tips she would give therapists to help them do well in interviews. Sue says she looks for confidence. She expects the therapists to do their research and have a clear understanding of the company. They also need to know what they want from the position. She looks for people who have a smart appearance and are well groomed, as they would be representing the brand.

I was interested to learn what qualities Sue looks for when she recruits for The Organic Pharmacy. She said a passion for the brand. Also, someone who leads an organic lifestyle, who is ambitious, and who is a strong team player with excellent customer-service skills.

I then asked Sue what staff could do to be promoted at work. She said that 100% commitment is what it takes to be recognised for a promotion and to further your career. For those wishing to move into management, Sue recommends always going the extra mile and being dedicated and hard-working.

Some therapists aren't confident about selling products, and I wanted to hear Sue's thoughts on the importance of selling, and whether she could offer tips to those therapists who struggle with sales. She believes that selling is a very important part of the job, as is customer care and understanding your client. She advises therapists to focus on their product knowledge and to make sure they know the ingredients and benefits of the products. 'Only then can you retail with confidence and recommend the most effective products to your clients.'

Matt Edmundson is an e-commerce entrepreneur and coach who founded The Jersey Beauty Company in 2006. I wanted to find out from Matt what it takes to be an entrepreneur and what skill set is needed. Matt said the answer is different depending on whom you speak to, as being an entrepreneur is deeply personal. Every entrepreneur he knows has a different reason for doing what they do, from wanting to change the world to wanting to be independent. Whatever the reason for doing it, it has to be enough to drive you, because it's one heck of a journey. Matt said that you'll have fun and highs, as well as fears and lows. To get through it, you have to have a deep-rooted belief in your cause (the reason why you're doing it) or you'll give up.

Matt writes about the 'art of venturing', and I asked him how we can make the most of every opportunity. He replied that opportunity is out there for all of us, just waiting to be discovered. There are hundreds, if not thousands, of opportunities for each one of us. Occasionally they're obvious, but more often than not opportunities play a little hard to get. Matt explained that opportunity likes to be courted, to be chased and pursued, because it wants to know how serious you are about finding it. Pursuit is proof of desire, and opportunity likes the pursuit. He explained that opportunities come in countless forms and disguises. They may be large, monster things or small, apparently insignificant things. Ugly or pretty, one thing is for sure – opportunities always lead to more opportunities. They never act alone or independently; they are all connected and entwined. They are a spider's web, a social network, a huge big family.

Matt reminds us that too often, we plan and talk ourselves out of action. A lot of life happens when you just have a go and see what happens. When an opportunity presents itself and it's within your power to try, do it. See what happens and then adjust your course accordingly. To do that, though, you have to be willing to fail (and be okay with failing).

I asked Matt about business lessons he's learned along the way, and he said that failure is an inevitable part of life and not to worry about it. Move on. Also, your 'killer idea' probably isn't as good as you think it is. Hard work is still the key to success. You have to think differently, stand out, and care about what's right.

Conclusion

In the screenplay *The Curious Case of Benjamin Button*, Eric Roth says:

> 'For what it's worth: it's never too late or, in my case, too early to be whoever you want to be. I hope you live a life you're proud of. If you find that you're not, I hope you have the courage to start all over again.'

Sometimes we beat ourselves up because we think we should be further ahead. Sometimes frustration takes over as we'd imagined our lives would be different. We overestimate what we can do in a year and underestimate what we can achieve in ten years.

We tend to forget how far we've come and don't celebrate enough the successes that we've had along the way. Starting today, celebrate the small wins. The little wins together get us where we want to go. When a small win happens, take a moment to be grateful and to celebrate.

Success doesn't happen overnight. It starts with a dream to achieve something. Getting to where you want to be requires effort. It requires putting in the hours. Ask any entrepreneur if the ride was easy – they will all tell you no. To be successful, you need to work hard, and you often need to work your way up from the bottom, doing jobs that aren't glamorous but that will help you move forward. Unicorn businesses (start-up companies with a valuation of $1 billion or more) seem to have become the norm, and we measure ourselves against them. They may appear to pop up overnight, but on average, it takes between seven and ten years to become an 'overnight success'. Success requires having your clients' needs at heart, a purpose-driven culture, and an incredible product or service that you're passionate about.

Set yourself goals. Make a start and just take the next step.

May your journey be filled with adventure.

Linda x

Acknowledgements

Special thanks to Chelsie Martone, Louise Phillips, Lorraine Hart, Josephine Wackett, Daniel Lees, Derek Mason, André Roodt, Jennifer Luyt, Chris Jones and David Rivington for your input and support.

The Author

Linda Hill was born and raised in Cape Town and graduated with a teaching degree from Stellenbosch University, where she majored in art. She added a public relations diploma to her credentials before moving to London in 1996. Linda decided to study something she has always been passionate about  and obtained the beauty industry's respected CIBTAC and CIDESCO diplomas.

Linda worked in London's most prestigious five-star hotels and spas before becoming a beauty lecturer teaching CIBTAC, CIDESCO, and NVQ students. Linda accepted the position of health and beauty manager at a chain of health clubs before taking on the role of acting general manager. In 2004, Linda set up an aesthetic and beauty recruitment agency. Her award-winning company helps job seekers and clients take their careers and businesses to the next level. Linda is an experienced speaker who has been invited to speak in Japan, South Africa, and the United Kingdom at various conferences and events. As a successful business owner, she receives invitations to share her entrepreneurial journey and inspire others to achieve success.

Linda Hill Recruitment®

www.lindahillrecruitment.co.uk

26406278R00113

Printed in Great Britain
by Amazon